# DROWNING IN SHALLOW WATER

Timothy L. Owings

SMYTH&HELWYS
PUBLISHING, INCORPORATED   MACON, GEORGIA

# DROWNING IN
### the hope of colossians for today's culture
# SHALLOW WATER

Timothy L. Owings

Smyth & Helwys Publishing, Inc.
6316 Peake Road
Macon, Georgia 31210-3960
1-800-747-3016
©2002 by Smyth & Helwys Publishing
All rights reserved.
Printed in the United States of America.

The paper used in this publication meets the minimum requirements of American National Standard for Information Sciences—Permanence of Paper for Printed Library Materials.

*Library of Congress Cataloging-in-Publication Data*

    Owings, Timothy.
    Drowning in shallow water: the hope of Colossians
    for today's culture/Timothy L. Owings.
    p.    cm.
    ISBN 1-57312-371-4 (pbk.)
    1. Bible. N. T. Colossians—Criticism, interpretation, etc. I. Title.
    BS2715.52 .O95 2002
    227'.7'06—dc21                                2001049837
                                                              CIP

To Kathie,
whose faithful love
and nourishing companionship
have often saved me from drowning

# Contents

**Acknowledgements** .................................................................ix
**Introduction** .........................................................................xi

**Chapter 1**: Drowning in Shallow Water ...............................1
  *(Colossians. 1:9-14)*

**Chapter 2**: New Age Undertow .........................................15
  *(Colossians 2:6-7)*

**Chapter 3**: The Danger of an Unholy Devotion ...............31
  *(Colossians 2:16-23)*

**Chapter 4**: The Beached Family .......................................45
  *(Colossians 3:18-4:1)*

**Chapter 5**: Beyond Wading Pool Friendships ...................61
  *(Colossians 4:7-18)*

**Chapter 6**: Who Is Jesus? .................................................75
  *(Colossians 1:15-20)*

**Chapter 7**: Rough Water Theology ..................................91
  *(Colossians 2:1-15)*

**Chapter 8**: Life Preserver Prayer ........................................................107
*(Colossians 1:3-8; 4:2-4)*

**Chapter 9**: Insiders and Outsiders ....................................................123
*(Colossians 4:5-6)*

**Chapter 10**: The New Community ..................................................139
*(Colossians 3:5-17)*

**Chapter 11**: Living at the Depths ....................................................159

**Appendix**..................................................................................171

# Acknowledgements

The deep waters of gratitude summon me to thank many for the support and encouragement generously given through the creation of this book. The lion's share of the manuscript had its genesis in print as my secretary of ten years, Dede Maddox, transcribed sermons, transforming them from sound to sight. To have such a devoted partner in ministry at the First Baptist Church of Augusta, Georgia, is God's daily gift both to me and the congregation.

The members and many television friends of First Baptist continue to offer embarrassingly extravagant affirmation of my preaching ministry. I am a blessed man to have such a warm and loving church to call me Pastor. That these chapters had their birth in sermons heard and remembered was all it took to motivate me to offer *Drowning in Shallow Water* to a wider audience. The people of God in Augusta are but one reminder of the larger community of faith both living and in God's eternal Kingdom who have been faithful to Christ across the ages.

A three-week sabbatical leave in May 1998 at Regent's Park College, Oxford, England, allowed me uninterrupted time to reflect, write, and live again through Paul's Letter to the Colossians. Living in Britain tends to remind me of George Bernard Shaw's observation that England and America are divided by a common language. What both societies presently have in common, however, is this rush to drown in life's inviting, shallow water. Both countries are emerging from a cultural modernity and civil religion bathed in Christianity. The past is not coming back, the future is yet undefined. Thus we live in a wasteland of cheap spiritual and relational satisfactions that are, at best, temporary. I am grateful to Dr. Paul Fiddes, Dr. John Weaver, Miss Fiona Floate, and other members of the Regent's Park community for warm hospitality and uncommon affirmation.

Gratitude is also due to Dr. Rob Nash and Shorter College, Rome, Georgia, for the invitation to be the 2001 Staley Lecturer. Offering the substance of four chapters of this book to the students and faculty at Shorter helped me refine my thinking in the affirming fire of gracious and insightful listeners. The Staley Foundation is to be commended for encouraging the interface of the mind and the spirit in the quest for meaningful expression of the Gospel in contemporary culture.

The many individuals at Smyth & Helwys Publishing have encouraged me to bring this work to print. Their careful attention to detail and passion about engaging the contemporary Christian community with the claims of the Gospel call me to do my best work. Whatever is excellent in the creation of this book is due in no small measure to their commitment both to me and readers everywhere.

Kathie is my life's companion in love and ministry. No man deserves such a devoted and giving mate. In her devotion, I have found strength, in her understanding courage, in her forgiveness grace, in her heart love. God indeed calls men and women to preach, to minister, to serve, to live among God's people as reminders of God's presence and God's faithfulness. I have not seen God, but I have experienced God in profound tenderness and uncommon courage in this my soul's mate for over 26 years. Whatever is true and good in me and in this work is, to a large extent, the evidence of her being my life's companion. Thank you Kathie for encouraging me to be my best self in serving the people of God.

# Introduction

Our children are telling us the truth. Made up, cool, together, looking good is but a cover-up masking the deep insecurities careening off the lonely walls of our lives. Children and teenagers cannot help but tell the truth. I know they stretch reality when backed into a "tell me the truth" corner. Wanting to avoid the punishment they fear is coming their way, most young people, up against being grounded, will lie about the party they attended, the alcohol that was or was not there, the speeding ticket warning a doting officer gave them instead of a citation, the poor grade they received on the biology exam.

Our children are telling us the truth about our culture. They can do nothing less. Their music, values, spending habits, and relationships all bear witness to the fact that the great American dream — whatever it was — is morphing into something else before our eyes. No one lives on Walton's Mountain anymore. The Cleavers never existed. The family that occupied the White House for most of the nineties is relationally sick. No place and no one is safe anymore. Grandparents are now categorized as step and biological, the adults living in the house are not married or will soon divorce, teachers no longer hug (too easy to misunderstand — touch must be "appropriate" or not at all), and God seems like a good idea but only in case of an emergency. We are drowning in shallow water.

This book is an attempt to name some of the maladies crippling our common humanity in these infant moments of the 21st century. Some books come to life in the throes of great passion; others limp out of a writer's own brokenness, loneliness, and fear. The pages that follow have erupted from my reading and rereading of Paul's Letter to the Colossians. In doing so, my own spiritual and relational struggles at midlife have collided with my calling to be a minister of the Gospel. By no means a scholar's volume, these chapters had their first gasps as sermons preached at the First Baptist Church of Augusta, Georgia. In the loving grip of a congregation that genuinely seeks to live out the demands of the Gospel even as it celebrates its wonder, I discovered Paul's diagnosis and treatment of our contemporary ills to be not only accurate, but highly redemptive.

The title — *Drowning in Shallow Water* — has a much more storied history. One of my mentors in ministry and partners in preaching has been Dr. William Augustus Jones, Jr., esteemed Pastor of Bethany Baptist Church in Brooklyn, New York. Through the providence and grace of God, I met Dr. Jones while a student at The Southern Baptist Theological Seminary in the early 1980s. Over four days, I marveled at the poetic genius of this African-American pastor and preacher. Soon, we met each other. In time, a friendship developed to such a degree that we have preached in each other's pulpits.

It has been more than ten years now since I asked my beloved friend if he would share with me the things about which he prayed most often. This is what he said: "I pray my mind doesn't die before my body; that I don't outlive my mourners; and that I don't drown in shallow water." The first two I understood completely; the last one still haunts me. When I asked Dr. Jones what he meant, he said he wanted to come to the end of his preaching ministry without embarrassing himself or his Lord. "You know Tim, some preachers don't know when to quit. They drown in shallow water."

The years have passed, but the haunting image of drowning in shallow water remains. Truth to tell, the image so haunted me that I did not know what to do with it other than to preach my way out of it. Now, in another context, Dr. Jones' seminal idea has come to life, first in sermons, and now in these pages.

Paul's Letter to the Colossians is often the stepchild of Bible study and preaching. The fact that it follows Paul's beloved letters to the Ephesians and Philippians is little help. That some scholars insist Colossians was not written by Paul — or worse, that it is only a downsized version of Ephesians — makes championing this letter all the more difficult. Aware of these potential obstacles, Colossians will not take second seat to any of Paul's other writings. In fact, the more I read its pithy, provocative four chapters, the more I hear the old Apostle speaking across two millennia to the infant moments of the 21st century.

So this book is offered as a conversation across 2000 years between two preachers. For my part, the reading of Colossians requires that I lift my eyes from the page in order to hear Paul describing what I see in contemporary culture. In four chapters, Paul wrestles with issues all too familiar to anyone living in the dawning, yawning minutes of the 21st century: family, trivial faith, angels, prayer, relationships, community, worship, and spirituality are but a few of the issues we meet in Colossians.

In my judgment, our society in general and the Christian church in particular are drowning in the shallow waters of trivial, even dangerous solutions to serious, life-threatening issues. We are intoxicated with feeling good about ourselves while refusing to act courageously to name, confront, and attempt to heal the pain in our society. We talk about the scourge of racism, but do little to build bridges with people of differing ethnic and/or religious backgrounds. We loudly blast the "secular, godless media" without having taken the first steps to have face-to-face dialogue with anyone who works in the media. Many express disdain and outright hostility for public education — no prayer in schools, God taken out of our classrooms, and so forth — while taking their children out of public schools in favor of private education or home schooling. Withdrawal from society is the order of the day — whether it's with our words, our actions, or our attitudes. The gay community, so needy of genuine Christian compassion, scares us. Government — always "big" and "greedy" — is only "us" personified in the people we elect. And yet, we fear all of the above from a safe, often suburban distance made ever wider by righteous rhetoric.

What are we doing? Simply put, we are condemning our society to an even riskier future without personally and spiritually engaging our society with the claims of the Gospel. We see the problems — violence in our schools, immorality, greed, materialism, feel-good spirituality, family dissolution — but we seem unwilling or unable to move beyond critical, self-righteous diagnosis to engaged, compassionate involvement. We are angry about society's profanely secular trajectory but our anger alienates nonbelievers, builds walls between believers, and is not resolved by any redemptive action-solution.

Yogi Berra was right: "You can observe a lot by looking around." And yet, many people of faith seem to be wading in society's shallow waters with their eyes wide shut. Yes, we take in the cultural scene in these early moments of the third millennium, but much of what we see is so obscene, so odious to our Christian sensitivities, that we react with disdain and at times outright belligerence. There's nothing wrong with our vision. It's our perception that is blurred, fuzzy, unfocused. In a word, we bump into what is fast becoming an American culture hostile not to faith in general, but to dogmatic, arrogant faith. So often, the Christian house of faith seems reluctant, if not afraid, to engage people within the culture. Instead, we blast our way out of the crowd; verbally and often politically attacking what we see as wrong. As with any blasting, offensive, militant campaign, casualties are many, both from within and without the believing community.

Two examples come immediately to mind. The first is the militant, often violent protest of abortion clinics in the United States. Don't get me wrong. I am an outspoken pro-life Christian who understands abortion as the ending of a life brought into being by the miracle of conception. Through the years, I have engaged people of all ages and from many differing positions on the abortion issue.

Even so, I find extremely offensive and morally wrong the bombing of abortion clinics and/or the murder of physicians who perform abortions. Such actions are in direct conflict with the teachings of both the Hebrew and Christian Scriptures. Addressing the abortion tragedy in our nation by blasting the practitioners of abortion takes the judgment of God into human hands and makes it nearly impossible for people of goodwill to debate openly the significant moral, spiritual, and ethical issues raised by the practice of abortion. What have the anti-abortion terrorists done? They have walked into the culture with their eyes wide shut, blasted the issue with violence and divisive rhetoric, and prohibited an intelligent, public conversation about the impact of abortion on our culture.

The American house is and most likely will continue to be divided over the sanctity of human life, birth control, and abortion. The ability to speak about these issues within the believing community has fared no better. Few issues within the Christian church are as emotionally charged as abortion. Whether one is Catholic, Baptist, Episcopal, Presbyterian, Lutheran, Methodist, charismatic, you name it, this issue divides the Christian house to such a degree that healthy conversation is almost impossible. Persons who love the Lord with equal fervor are vilified in private and attacked in public because they understand the abortion issue from differing perspectives. There is a great gulf fixed that seems uncrossable.

Christians are positioned by those outside the believing community as irrational, militant, obtuse, even dangerous, so much so that the radical, violent fringe is postured as embracing the position of all Christians. From inside the Church house, we sit in lonely pews glaring at each other, whispering destructive clichés about the other group's narrow-mindedness or liberalism as the case may be. Lesslie Newbigin — speaking as an observant insider — put his pen point on the problem. "The words 'liberal' and 'fundamentalist' are freely used among us as terms of abuse and contempt. In this mutual hostility, which is so damaging to the Church's witness, we are in danger of evading the real issues on which the gospel must challenge our culture. It is obvious that this damaging split in the life of the Church is only one manifestation of the much deeper split which runs through the whole of our culture."[1] The Church, harpooned from without and stared down from within, seems impotent. We are drowning in shallow water.

A second example would be the intense debate in our society about homosexuality. In 1999, the Georgia Baptist Convention withdrew fellowship from two Atlanta churches who have chosen to bless same sex unions and ordain openly gay persons to ministry. My understanding of the Bible will not permit me as a minister to bless a same sex union or to ordain an individual to ministry who is living the homosexual lifestyle.

So where are we? Politically, the reality in which we live insures equal rights to all persons under the Constitution. To discriminate against homosexuals is un-American because it violates our national charter. Spiritually, Jesus has no quarter with any movement to exclude any person from the grace of God. Relationally, both the heterosexual majority and the homosexual minority in 21st century America struggle to find open, honest ways to accept each other as citizens with equal rights and

God-given dignity. From the secular culture's side of the aisle, the Georgia Baptist Convention's decision stirred such heated rhetoric in the press that those outside the Christian community have little choice but to assume all Baptists are anti-gay. The position taken by the Convention has made it even more difficult today to engage the gay community — both Christian and non-Christian — in healthy dialogue about homosexuality. Jerry Falwell is to be commended for having invited a large delegation of gay Christians to Thomas Road Baptist Church in Lynchburg, Virginia for open conversation and prayer about inclusion of and ministry to gay persons within and without the church.

From inside the Baptist house, I can say firsthand the Georgia Baptist Convention's decision has caused no small amount of pain in the lives of many church members who are gay or have adult gay children. Are homosexuals not welcome in our churches? Can we not have an open, honest conversation about homosexuality within the church? Unfortunately, the actions of a denomination bear witness to the fact we are walking through society with our eyes wide shut. We have named issues — abortion, homosexuality, and so forth — but we seem unable or unwilling to have dialogue, much less relationship, with individuals or groups whose position differs from our own. To make matters worse, convictions thoughtful Christians hold within the Church about these hot-button issues can be radically opposite. Yes, there are pro-life and pro-choice, pro-gay lifestyle and anti-gay lifestyle, pro-capital punishment and anti-capital punishment beliefs in the Christian house. So what do we do? How do we hold with integrity our convictions while reaching out to those with whom we disagree?

Perhaps you know the popular Christian song, "Open our eyes, Lord; We want to see Jesus; to reach out and touch him; to say that we love him. Open our ears, Lord, and help us to listen; Open our eyes, Lord; we want to see Jesus." In my judgment, the great need facing the Christian family in the 2000s is to see Jesus first. We can only then look at issues as they can be seen through the life, the words, the face, the Gospel of our Lord. For as long as I can remember, both conservative and liberal expressions of Christian faith have looked at issues first and Jesus second, or third, or later.

What do I mean? Quite simply, we are facing nothing less than the marginalization of the Christian faith in an increasingly secular and narcissistic culture. The church house, the church's minister, the church's values are not so much attacked today as they are simply ignored. The politically correct mantra of our society is now too sophisticated to attack Christians — everyone's view is valid, isn't it? Instead – glimpsed more in larger cities – churches, their ministers, and their members are seen as relics of a bygone era. Believers "go to church" but little of church goes anywhere. An article a couple of years ago in *The Wall Street Journal* with the catchy title "The Holidays Get Religion," chronicled the increase in attendance at worship services as the year 2000 neared. Writer Lisa Miller, in dialogue with both lay and professional interviewees, noted, "These [people reconnecting with organized religion] aren't zealots hunkering down for the end of the world. They are ordinary people searching for a connection with God." Indeed. The desired "connection with God" is no new preferred outcome for people wandering into a house of worship. The question gnawing at my soul is: What difference does one's connection with God make in personal relationships, shared community values, ministry to our society's marginalized and ignored?

Truth to tell, Christians – seeing the culture with eyes wide shut – have engaged the issues we believe are destroying society. We have attacked the abortionists, the homosexuals, big government, racial inequality, alcohol and illegal drugs, teen pregnancy, and other challenging issues all the while ignoring conversation about Jesus; his life, his values, his power to change lives. We do so, repeatedly, to our peril.

The Gospel of Mark records an intriguing story from Jesus' life about an encounter he had one day with a blind man (Mark 8:22-26). Jesus is in the town of Bethsaida, on the northwest shore of the Sea of Galilee. A group of people brought a blind man to Jesus and asked that he be healed. Jesus takes the blind man out of the village by the hand, no doubt to give them both a moment of privacy. Our Lord takes his hands, touches the man's eyes, and asks, "Can you see anything?" To which the man replies, surprisingly, "I can see people, but they look like trees, walking." Jesus repeats the gesture, touching his eyes a second time. Immediately, profoundly, the man saw "everything clearly." Even so, the story has a strange ending. Rather than inviting the now-seeing man to follow him or even to go into Bethsaida and tell his story, Jesus sends the man away, forbidding him to go into the village. Could it be the twice-touched man is unprepared to be a witness? Seeing everything clearly may not be enough.

What's happening in this story? For starters, let's step back and take a larger look at the context. This healing in Mark comes two verses before we read the confession of Simon Peter at Caesarea Philippi – "You are the Christ!" At that moment, Jesus praised his number one disciple and then proceeded to tell him and the 12 that he would be betrayed, rejected, crucified, and killed in Jerusalem. Instantly, Peter objected: "This will never happen to you!" To which Jesus replied, "Get behind me Satan!" From this pivotal point in Mark, Jesus will predict his death and resurrection another two times as he leads the disciples from Galilee in the north to the Holy City in the south, there to endure a bloody cross alone.

Read further in Mark – go to Mark 10:46-52. Immediately before Jesus and the disciples arrive in Jerusalem, another blind man is healed, this time in Jericho, at the beginning of the steep ascent to the City. This time, the blind man confesses Jesus to be "Son of David" prior to receiving his sight. In other words, the second blind man sees spiritually before he sees physically. At Jesus' touch, he receives his sight and, Mark adds, "follows him on the way."

Two blind men, two healings, two different situations. In my judgment, the contemporary church is much like the not-quite-seeing man in Bethsaida. We have had a first touch from Jesus – enough to save us? Give us spiritual confidence? Provide us with enough "answers" to be obnoxious? – but have gone off with blurred vision, leaving Jesus to go south to a cross we'd rather avoid. Like Peter, we protest Jesus' suffering and death, knowing such sacrifice puts us much too close to the obituaries. So what do we do? We attack our society's ills, sins, failings, immoralities, darkness without the One who alone is life. We start fires of protest, fires that have much heat, but little light.

Only a re-introduction to Jesus can save us from further marginalization by the very society we say we want to impact. Only Jesus can save us from our dis-engaged zealotry and self-righteousness. Only Jesus can give us the relational tools we need to reach across the moral and spiritual abyss separating our culture from the believing community whose mission is to save, heal, reconcile, recreate. Only Jesus' kind of understanding and acceptance offers any hope of breaking down the barriers within and without the Church. We must re-connect with Jesus. But how?

Paul's Letter to the Colossians gives us a starting point for navigating the shallow waters of our time. Our vision is blurred without divine healing. Only Jesus can touch our eyes and enable us to see his face of sacrificial love and grace. Both believers and unbelievers are drowning in the trivialities of our day. What is needed is clear vision and courageous hearts to live in the deep waters of authentic, biblical faith that is hard wired to Jesus Christ and sensitive to people for whom Jesus died and rose again. In my own experience, I have come near to drowning in so many shallow waters. My only hope of being rescued – our only hope – is in re-connecting with Jesus Christ: his heart, his compassion, his way of reaching across barriers and building redemptive relationships.

So open the tiny letter Paul wrote to the Colossians nearly 2000 years ago. Sit down, read it in one sitting. Then go with me through this book and listen to one inspired by God long ago who tells us we are in danger of a shallow water drowning while showing us the way to live fully in the deep, nourishing grace of God.

## Notes

[1] Lesslie Newbigin, *Truth to Tell: The Gospel as Public Truth* (Grand Rapids: William B. Eerdmans Publishing Company, 1991) 41-42.

# Drowning in Shallow Water

> For this reason, since the day we heard it, we have not ceased praying for you and asking that you may be filled with the knowledge of God's will in all spiritual wisdom and understanding, so that you may lead lives worthy of the Lord, fully pleasing to him, as you bear fruit in every good work and as you grow in the knowledge of God. May you be made strong with all strength that comes from his glorious power, and may you be prepared to endure everything with patience, while joyfully giving thanks to the Father, who has enabled you to share in the inheritance of the saints in light. He has rescued us from the power of darkness and transferred us into the kingdom of his beloved Son, in whom we have redemption, the forgiveness of sins. (Col 1:9-14)

Contemporary society is drowning in shallow water. If all of us could speak, we might confess from some deeper cavern of our souls that, in many ways, we are a fearful people. There seems to be loose in our individual and collective lives this great fear — could I say terror? — that the things to which we are giving our time, money, influence are, in fact, less than worthy pursuits. Are we drowning in shallow water? One of the more pressing issues seems to be that we do not know how to save ourselves, much less our society, from an uncertain future. Actually, we seem fidgety, even fretful over any number of predicted futures while, at the same time, being incurably nostalgic about the imagined past. Another indicator of our dilemma is our collective neurosis about the economy, all the while being told by Wall Street's pundits "it's the best in 30 years." And yes, to make the obvious plain, we are almost immobilized with guilt over the rearing of our children, having in many cases compromised the integrity of home for some as yet unrealized benefit "out there" somewhere. In a word, all of us are gasping for spiritual air in the churning waters of postmodern America.

The shallow water in which we are drowning laps around the ankles of our personal lives, every social structure, and even the community of faith. In these dawning moments of the third millennium, we are asking ourselves gnawing questions like: What of life really endures? What is it that is really important? Am I giving my so-called life to that which will out last my years? At the end of the day — my life? — did I give myself to that which ennobled others and brought glory to God? When we come to the end of life's journey and look back, I believe all of us want to answer that question with a satisfying "Yes."

At the same time, we seem afraid even to ask more troubling questions like: Did I give my life to trivial pursuits, to causes and work and values that do not endure? Then again, all of us are not sure how we plan to answer this one: Have I paid for life with cheap currency only to discover too late that life is far more valuable than I imagined?

We all have these fears, do we not? When we get to the end of our lives, will we be embarrassed by what we see? If that's not our greatest fear, it surely is near the top of the list. The words of a Christian popular song ask a very good question: "Will those who come behind us find us faithful?" We are not sure. In moments of transparent honesty, we are afraid to ask these and other difficult questions. Perhaps we are drowning in shallow water.

Cruise into any grocery store today, pick up a few items, and make your way to the check-out counter. Before you can place your purchases on the conveyor, faster than you can say "debit card," you find yourself surrounded by a gang of tabloid thugs. Pick up the headlines and feast your soul-hungry eyes on "the untold stories" of people you would rather forget. Do you know why they market the tabloids at the check out counter? For one reason, marketing mavens call them "impulse items." The headlines "grab you" while you are waiting your turn to check out. Many, indeed, do "check out." Next time you are there, surrounded by those bizarre headline bullies, ask, "How many are drowning in shallow water, living life by tabloid?" Andrew Walker, in his provocative book *Telling the Story*, accurately describes the need of so many today to find themselves by either publicly exposing their failures — think guests on shows like Jerry Springer or Montel Williams — or who use their own failures as a launching pad for talk show fame — think Oprah Winfrey. Walker writes: "If we cannot feel better, then perhaps we can become famous through our therapeutic failings. Oprah Winfrey is the symbol of triumph through dysfunction. Once we craved functional adequacy, now we flout our inadequacy."[1] The once "normal" has become exception to some, bizarre to others. Now, the more weird it can appear, the more likely we are to leer like voyeurs into the seedy, shallow lives of people we would not like as next door neighbors. Tabloid television sells, advertisers know it, and American television audiences are buying.

With the advent of the information super highway, tabloid-like internet wallpaper spams your screen with the weird, lurid, even pornographic. Add to this psychic hot lines at $3.95 a minute, tarot card stupidity, and revolving door marriages and families and, before any of us can shout "Stop!", we have a society drowning in shallow water. What gives?

Where once we could turn to elected officials locally and nationally, now such options seem at best an exercise in wishful thinking. The political scene offers little encouragement. From President to precinct worker, the information age offers us more water without additional depth. Money laundering, alleged sexual impropriety, truth squeezing and position shifting are but a few of the goods trafficked in the political marketplace. Politically speaking, we are drowning in information, unable to connect it all together, much less get it all together. We have much, all the while terribly frightened about the prospects of being less.

Is there hope and help for this "new age" awash in turbulent, dangerous but shallow waters? A few years ago, I spent six weeks in Britain. One of the blessings of being in Britain for such an extended stay was escaping the United States gossip mongers. Nevertheless, it did not take me long to learn the British have out-tabloided us. They have their own scandal mills, cranking out the insipid and inane scribblings of hungry journalists. Not to shock you, but the British have tabloid papers that make ours look mild. After returning to the States, I went to the grocery store a couple of times and there, at the check-out line, were familiar friends: *The Inquirer* and *The Star*. I thought to myself, "How refreshing to come back to America and find a weekly tabloid rather than a daily." That's right, the Brits have daily tabloids. You can plunk down your pence every day, and drown all over again in stories of sex, bribery, extortion, murder, and worse.

The question lingers: Are we surrounding our minds with and giving our passions to all kinds of information and data that cannot lift us to higher levels of existence? In my judgment, many today, without their conscious consent, are allowing the shallow waters of trivial pursuits to drown their higher instincts in low thinking and even lower living. What is the God-destined, life-affirming purpose for which God created us?

The Bible does not leave us without help or hope. In fact, the Bible candidly acknowledges the fact that, left to itself, humankind will drown in the shallowest of shore-lapping waters. One tiny book in the New Testament reads with eerie precision in diagnosing our current predicament. Paul's Letter to the Colossians is a brief letter from the mid-first century that points with laser precision to these early third millennium moments. To read Colossians from a modern translation of the Bible is chilling. My reading and rereading of this tiny letter leaves me with the feeling that Paul could have penned the letter last week.

In a nutshell, Paul wrote to a first century congregation troubled by many things. In the pages that follow, I invite you to pick up this incredible document and let Paul's letter call you to live in faith's deeper waters. The good news, for all of with deep need but with shallow time, is you can read all four chapters in less than fifteen minutes. You may find, as I have, that Paul is speaking directly to us who are tiptoeing into a new century. In provocative prose, he addresses issues that faced a first century Christian church with such accuracy, we who read it today must remind ourselves the document is nearly 2000 years old.

One of the issues that falls out of the text of Colossians is the macro concern that life has more in it than we are as yet prepared to admit. More is going on in relationships, in families, in individual lives, in the struggles to be simply present and civil to others than the press could possibly report. Paul reminded the Colossians of the ominous, frightening truth that, if we are not careful, we will drown in the shallow waters of our age. In the chapters that follow, we will examine things like the "new age" movement, angels, friendship, job responsibility, temptation, family, prayer, the church, and worship. Right now, however, I invite you to prepare for the journey by looking at Paul's prayer offered on behalf of the Colossians.

## A Prayer for Spiritual Depth

The simple but profound prayer of Colossians 1:9-14, offered by an imprisoned Christian preacher nearly 2000 years ago, reveals at least five available resources that can keep us from drowning in shallow water. Not only are these resources within our reach, but they have in them the power to enable us to move out into the depths of life.

**"Be Filled with the Knowledge of God's Will"**

While doing a sabbatical study leave at Oxford, I rummaged around for a few hours in one of the great repositories of knowledge in the world, the Bodleian Library at Oxford University. It is a treasure trove containing much of the accumulated knowledge of humankind. Over five and a half million volumes comprise the collection of what is affectionately called at Oxford, "the Bod." I'm told there is one section of the Bodleian — the Duke Humphery's Library — that doesn't have a book in it published after 1640. We are dealing here with a very old collection of knowledge that continues to grow day by day.

When I had finished my work for the day, I walked across the street from the Bodleian to Blackwell's Bookstore. Now Blackwell's has only a half million volumes for sale on the shelves. To be honest, Blackwell's is so large, it makes Books-A-Million look like a newsstand. I'm told, jokingly of course, that people have died in Blackwell's and haven't been found for days.

Having gone into the Bodleian Library and used its resources and made a couple of pilgrimages to Blackwell's to spend a few pounds, I came to a comforting realization that no one — not me, you, others, or all of us together — is capable of putting his or her mental arms around all that humankind has learned. It is a humbling experience to walk thoughtfully through stacks of books, spanning centuries, bearing witness to humankind's incredible passion for learning.

We are fond of calling this era of human history "the information age." We pride ourselves on being able to have immediate access to all manner of data from around the world. Is it not ironic that this information age, filled with the knowledge of so much, is actually an age in which we are drowning from a lack of knowledge of the will of God? This scarcity of knowing God's will is, in fact, leading to spiritual and relational death in our lives, our families, and so many of our relationships. No longer is it public knowledge that God has a standard by which life can positively and joyfully be lived. Historians now suggest, with no small degree of dissent from other quarters of academia, that there has never been a time when such public knowledge existed. What we once believed was "Christian America" we know now to have been more imaginary than fact. Even so, many have memories, albeit from childhood, of a community whose value system was largely predicated upon the morality one finds in the Hebrew and Christian Bible.

How ironic. Our age seems eager to believe that knowledge alone is able to save us from all manner of shallow water drownings. To be honest, knowledge is neither moral nor immoral, godly nor atheistic; it has no power apart from the authority and place we give it in our lives. From this prayer, we can see that Paul, no puny intellect in his own right, was not down on learning. Rather, he was lifting up the greater imperative that, with all our learning, we fill our lives with the knowledge of the will of God. Whether fifteen or fifty, a high school graduate or a highly educated scholar, the most important questions we can ask are: How could my life bring glory to God today and in the tomorrows that meet me each morning? What would be God's will for my life in the circumstances I face? What would ennoble others with the grace of God? What words could I speak that would bless others with the love of God? What influence could I give? What time could I spend deepening my life and the lives of others? If we have any hope of avoiding a shallow water drowning, we would be wise to hear and follow Paul's wise counsel: Fill your life with the knowledge of the will of God. What would God's will be for my life? Ask questions like these and ask them often.

At her funeral, I called her "St. Frances" of Augusta. Her name was Frances Hardin. She was one of God's unique and significant gifts to the people of First Baptist Church and our larger community. I was fond of Frances for so many reasons: she served on the Pastor Search Committee that brought me to Augusta, she had a keen mind, she refused to accept any thinking or theology that cheapened human life or discriminated against any human being, and she genuinely loved me with all my failings and inconsistencies.

In our congregation, where Frances served as a deacon, she gave her life after retirement from the public schools to the Conversational English ministry of the church. Each year, some 200 foreign nationals, many of them women, come to our church to learn English as a second language. Staffed by dozens of teachers and workers, the Conversational English ministry of First Baptist Church is an outreach expression of the love of God. We teach our foreign guests English; we introduce them to Jesus Christ and the Gospel.

Suddenly, in the fall of 1996, Frances Hardin died of an aneurysm. When the initial shock of her death hit me and others in our Church, the first question that came to most of our minds was: Who will now give leadership to the Conversational English ministry? Within a few days, many came forward to fill the gaping, empty place left by Frances' death. Today, the ministry goes on and is stronger because Frances and so many others before her gave good gifts to share the love of Christ through the medium of teaching.

I still can not help think about Frances and what she could have done with her life after retirement. A widow of many years prior to her retirement from full-time employment, she could have spent her last years in traveling, playing bridge with her friends, reading books, spoiling her precious grandchildren, and doing her own thing. Had she done so, no one would have thought anything of it. Retirement, as we have come to imagine it, is God's gift to "do with as I please," is it not? Frances thought otherwise. She decided that travel, family, grandchildren, music, and an active social life did not have to exclude Christian service. She decided her life still had much to give to God and others. Her decision was to serve actively and generously until God called her home. I am so grateful she did. Literally thousands of Conversational English graduates are grateful she did. A church that still misses her laughter, her service, her wisdom, and her encouragement is grateful she did. And what of Frances' testimony still speaks?

We who claim to "know" Christ would be wise to fill our lives with the knowledge of his will. Such knowledge will not let us expend our life's resources, time, or talents only on ourselves. Deeper water calls us to other investments of God's good gifts.

**"Lead lives worthy of the Lord"**

As I mentioned earlier, the British have out-tabloided us. After returning from England, I told a man in our church who happens to be in the newspaper business, he ought to go to Britain because they really know what to do with newsprint. They read newspapers. They read everything, much of it tabloid stupidity.

I had an experience shortly before leaving Oxford at the college where I stayed, Regent's Park College. There was a party taking place in the quadrangle of the college one evening. The lacrosse teams from the University had requisitioned the quadrangle of Regent's Park for a party. They have a rather large garden area in which you could have an outdoor party and they secured that space to do so. I was interested to learn that many of the people who make up the lacrosse teams at Oxford are from Britain's upper crust socially and economically.

As they gathered for their party in the quad, I went upstairs to read the newspaper — I told you they had a zillion of them. Upstairs, looking over the quad, were a group of Oxford students not attending the party down on the lawn. I wish you could have heard the epithets, the sneers, the language used by the people upstairs referring to the so-called aristocracy attending the party. I got an insight into the division within British society I could not have had any other way but by observing that phenomenon taking place. The "have not's" looking down their noses at those whom they believed were the "haves," making all kinds of unpleasant comments about them. I was reminded in that moment that I often do the same thing privately, sometimes publicly, and so do you.

What is it to which you give your life that is worthy of the Lord, pleasing him? So much of what we do only pleases ourselves in a vain attempt to get others to look. Paul said, "Live a life worthy of the Lord pleasing him." Seek to please God. The Westminster Confession, to my knowledge, has not been rescinded. The opening line says, "The chief end of man is to glorify God and to enjoy Him forever." The archaic, sexist language aside, humankind's supreme purpose is found in pleasing God. It seems to me that if we are going to avoid a shallow water drowning, it behooves us to live a life worthy of the Lord. What would happen if we saw our lives as a benediction to the grace of God or as a witness to the glory, love, and grace of God? Choose a lifestyle that brings glory to God and you greatly reduce the risk of drowning in the shallow waters of this age.

**"Bear fruit in every good work"**

The church has been called a "Do-Gooder" society. Guilty as charged! We are a society compelled by grace to do good. Paul, writing to the Ephesians, said that grace works within us so that good works flow from us (Eph 2:10). James said to those who read his letter that we are to "be doers of the word and not hearers only" (James 1:22). Yes, the church is a "Do-Gooder" society.

And yet so often we communicate this amorphous, undefined admonition to our children to "be good." I said it to my children when they were young and you probably did as well — "Now be good." When we heard that order as children, we did not know what it meant, but we knew it meant something serious. Be good. As best I can decipher those two words, I believe they mean "do not misbehave, don't get in trouble, keep your nose clean, be thoughtful."

Paul seems to suggest that we could spend our whole lives "being good" and never *do* good. The grace of God and only the grace of God is that which makes us good. The only way we can be good is by the grace of God. But having received and accepted with grateful arms that grace, we are to do good. We are to bear fruit in life. Our lives are made new in Christ to be trees laden with the evidence of the grace of God. Clearly Paul believed the doing of good deepened a life committed to Christ. "Bear fruit in every good work." In another chapter, we will explore this phrase in more detail as we consider Paul's profile of a Christian insider.

**"Be made strong with all the strength that comes from his glorious power"**

The word "power" always draws a crowd. The shallow water realities in which most live today associate power with things like money, success, sexual conquest, political influence, and insider information. The Christian definition of power is radically different. Power, so defined by Jesus Christ, is only found in servanthood, self-giving, and sacrifice. In Christ, we do not face life's churning seas without God's presence and God's grace. And yet I sense there is a gnawing suspicion among contemporary believers born of forgotten faith that we who follow Christ are nothing more than a whining, impotent, powerless community. Have we forgotten that the God who loves us and who is saving us in Jesus Christ is able, ready, willing, and wanting to empower us with new life that we might be God's people?

Paul said that if we would realize this we would be strengthened with God's glorious might equipping us with gifts of endurance and patience. Perhaps we lack a sense of power, a sense of competence today as believers because we fail to rely on Christ. I sense among Christian people, both in Britain and the United States, a sense of spiritual helplessness before the seemingly pernicious social and relational maladies we face. We read about the political and economic problems of far off places like Northern Ireland, Indonesia, Russia, the Ukraine, and what may best be called "the hot spot of the week." For us, such problems seem almost surreal. And yet, for people living through such cataclysmic upheaval, these issues are of a life and death nature.

What we in the secure confines of the United States do not often hear is that Christian believers in these troubled places — Baptists, Anglicans, Pentecostals, Methodists, Presbyterians, and others — often have a sense of competence, strength, even confidence, that is born of God. Rather than fretting and fearing the "what if's" of the future, our brothers and sisters in faith have learned what only difficulty seems to be able to teach us. Trusting God is the only response that addresses the crippling reality of fear. That same confidence could be God's gift to us who seem to be drowning in the shallow waters of our materialistic culture.

On two or three occasions, I have attended Evensong at some of the college chapels in Oxford. The most worshipful place for me is the chapel of New College. New College, Oxford was founded in 1379. That's *New* College — *1379.* When I first attended evensong there, I sat in the choir stalls with other worshipers who were all strangers to me. During the worship service, as prayers were offered, the psalms chanted, the anthem sung, I looked to my right and there towering above the chapel was a reredos in solid limestone, some forty or fifty feet high, in which were carved the apostles, prophets, martyrs, and heroes of the faith. As I turned from looking at that magnificent remembrance of those who have gone before us, my eyes looked up toward the ceiling and there I noticed, carved in the dark wood of that 500 year old chapel, huge spread angels over the choir. In that moment, I was reminded that those who went before us, those who have gone and given their lives and their witness did so, not by themselves, but empowered by the very presence and love of God that is ever present to us as those angels hover over the worshipers in the chapel of New College.

Want to avoid a shallow water drowning? Lean your life on the strength and power of God. God is faithful. We who are called the people of God have been bought with a price, the precious blood of Christ. God has empowered us in Christ to live and to be God's promise and presence to others. Such a confidence can deliver us from drowning in shallow water.

### "Give thanks to the Father"

Colossians has much to teach us about gratitude. In fact, we will be revisiting this theme often in our journey through the letter. Here, at the beginning of Colossians, Paul said we are to live "giving thanks to the Father, who has enabled you to share in the inheritance of the saints in light." Gratitude is to be the crowning virtue in our lives. For Paul, gratitude is not only the last word, it is also the first word and only one of a handful of enduring words (cf. Col 2:6; 3:15, 17; 4:2). Earlier in the first chapter of Colossians, Paul told the church that he and Timothy "always thank God" for the faithfulness of the Colossian believers. Gratitude can protect us from drowning in shallow water. Paul encouraged the Colossians to find gratitude to be the deep well of spiritual vitality. Shallowness in this age — shallowness in this moment of our lives — may be so threatening because we have turned all the lights in the house on ourselves. We have forgotten to be people of thanks.

Persons who live with gratitude live with power. To live in this moment in human history, though we think it the worst of times, is to live in an age not unlike others that have preceded it. Every age of human history has faced its own struggles, crises, and lurking despair. Paul's strong word to the Colossians is a lightening strike across the centuries to us. We need not face this moment without the strength, power, and presence of God. None of us from the youngest to the oldest need be a fatality in the raging surf of this crazy moment of history.

In the library of Regent's Park College is a portrait of John Bunyan, author of *Pilgrim's Progress*. In 1660, Charles II came to the throne and the monarchy was restored in Britain. That same year, John Bunyan was imprisoned in Bedford jail for preaching the Gospel without a license. For the next twelve years, Bunyan languished in Bedford jail. For murder? Robbery? Felony? No! For preaching without a license. Twelve years in Bedford jail. Finally the authorities released him in 1672. You know what he did? He went right back to the Baptist church in Bedford and continued his preaching. Three years later, they threw him back in Bedford jail. Not until 1678 did Bunyan write *Pilgrim's Progress*. Note the sequence of events in his life. The monumental testimony of faith and towering literary achievement *Pilgrim's Progress* was not written during his first twelve years of incarceration, nor in freedom's fresh air after being released from jail when he returned to his pulpit. Not until Bunyan was thrown back in jail a second time, did he write that immortal classic.

I remind you of that snippet of history for one reason. John Bunyan and every fore-parent of faith before him and after him who lived with a sense of depth and purpose in life was able to do so for one reason: they deeply believed that what they said, what they believed, and how they lived really mattered to God and to others. What would happen in our day, in our circumstances, if we believed the same thing?

Drowning in shallow water? Wondering if all you are doing and all you believe really makes any difference? Hear God's good word. Swim out into the depths and know the power and the promise of the living Christ.

## Prayer

Almighty God, by whose power all creation came into being and in whose grace all reality will find its destiny, we bow our lives before your presence to worship and adore you as the only being worthy of our praise. O God, how we love you.

With audacious confidence in your mercy, we ask forgiveness for all we have done that cheapens our lives and mocks your name. Created to swim in the deep waters of your love, we are drowning in the shallow waters of self-serving sin and immature behaviors. Given the gift of language, we too often use words to wound others made in your image rather than using the glory of language to bless and ennoble others with whom we share the precious gift of life. We have lived with little sense of spiritual depth.

Forgive us, we pray. Open our ears to hear again your invitation to live far away from life's shallow waters. There is so much you have for us if we would dare to live boldly and faithfully and generously.

God of all grace, look with mercy upon us as we look with hope upon you. This we pray through Jesus Christ, whose cross is our salvation and whose resurrection is our life. Amen.

## Note

[1] Andrew Walker, *Telling the Story: Gospel, Mission and Culture* (London: SPCK, 1996), 181.

# New Age Undertow

As you therefore have received Christ Jesus the Lord, continue to live your lives in him, rooted in the faith, just as you were taught, abounding in the thanksgiving. See to it that no one takes you captive through philosophy and empty deceit, according to human tradition, according to the elemental spirits of the universe, and not according to Christ. For in him the whole fullness of deity dwells bodily, and you have come to fullness in him, who is the head of every ruler and authority. In him also you were circumcised with a spiritual circumcision, by putting off the body of the flesh in the circumcision of Christ; when you were buried with him in baptism, you were also raised with him through the faith in the power of God, who raised him from the dead. And when you were dead in trespasses and the uncircumcision of your flesh, God made you alive together with him, when he forgave us all our trespasses, erasing the record that stood against us with its legal demands. He set this aside, nailing it to the cross. He disarmed the rulers and authorities and made a public example of them, triumphing over them in it. (Col 2:6-15)

Sunrise over the third millennium, though seemingly placid and promising, is deceptive and spiritually dangerous. Bright hope for a "new age" of human tolerance, empowered by diversity and glorying in pluralism is anything but simple. Look beneath the gently rolling swells, where the world's major religious traditions traffic in ideas, theology, and activism and you will discover a churning, deadly undertow threatening all but the most skilled of swimmers. We live today lulled into a false security by a mantra that suggests that any faith is good faith. What you believe is not as important as *that* you believe: any spirituality that makes you feel whole, connected, empowered, dare I say "alive," is good and ultimately right. But is it?

Much ink has flowed among mainline Christians groups in the last decade over the threat of what is called the "New Age Movement." If the truth were known, what we call the New Age Movement has been around longer than the Bible. In fact, the years in which the New Testament was written (AD 50–100) witnessed a vital and dynamic spiritual movement sweep the Roman Empire that felt and acted exactly like the contemporary New Age Movement. New Testament scholars call this old-New Age phenomenon "Gnosticism." Like present-day New Agers, the first century version had no particular religious home. Gnosticism leaked into Judaism, Christianity, and the dozens of Greco-Roman pagan religions populating the ancient landscape. Put another way, Gnosticism moved horizontally across religious lines, coloring the varied theological tenets of all religions with new and provocative ideas.

For example, first century gnostic thought suggested that Jesus Christ was not fully human. Those who held this view believed all reality was in fact created by an evil God one meets in the pages of the Hebrew Bible. The first century New Agers reasoned this evil deity created evil matter. Why else would there be unexplainable tragedy, natural disasters, even death? Hence, all that is material is corrupt and beyond redemption. Jesus, as their reasoning went, could not possibly be human because human flesh was and is, by definition, evil. For many, this made sense; many first century Christians, Jews, and adherents to other religions bought into the gnostic-New Age explanation–interpretation of life.

How did it work? These first century New Agers tended to express their beliefs in one of two ways. They either became extremely ascetic, denying themselves all physical comfort and pleasure, or they became morally promiscuous, indulging in all manner of sensuality. Put another way, Christians infected with Gnosticism either denied their physical needs (the body is evil), or caved in to every "natural" desire (since my soul is redeemed, I can do what I please with my body). Paul addressed the former camp — let's call them the "denyers" — in his Letter to the

Colossians when he scolded them for suggesting "denial" was a Christian requirement (Col 2:20-23). On the other hand, he condemned the "do-as-you-feel" group — let's call them the "indulgers" — for missing the Christian truth that our bodies and our souls are, in fact, one reality; how we live is bonded to who we are (see Phil 3:17–4:1). As the infant Church of the first century became a toddling child in the second and third centuries, Gnosticism grew in persuasive power. Many Christian communities succumbed to it's allure.[1]

Not surprisingly, both expressions of first century Gnosticism survive in the present-day New Age Movement. The "denyers" — all-matter-is-evil — reject materialism in any form, insisting simplicity is the best way to find spiritual peace. On the other side of the aisle, the "indulgers" — do-what-you-feel — preach a gospel of pleasure, hedonism, and sublime earthly joys as the supreme way to do life. Make no mistake about it: both expressions of first century Gnosticism–New Age thinking are pervasive in contemporary life.

Like our first century brothers and sisters, today's Christian believers are not immune to the horizontal invasion of the New Agers. Like the gnostics of old, one way believers today drown in shallow water is to be sucked under the surf by what I call the New Age undertow. I grew up in South Florida. There, along the southeastern coast of the United States, the waves pound the beach with an unrelenting cadence. If you like placid beaches, go to the west coast of Florida, don't come to Miami. Simply put, from the Keys to Miami and West Palm on up toward Cocoa Beach, the waves often pummel the eastern shore of Florida with great power.

Often, when I would go to the beach as a child, there would be a warning posted: "Beware of the undertow." I knew what that meant: Stay close to the shore. Because if you go too far out, the pounding surf creates a subsurface, churning undertow invisible on the surface. The sea near to shore may look normal, but underneath that water is a current that can sweep you out to sea and even death.

There is a current beneath the gently rolling sea of religious life today. It is taking many people out to sea to spiritual irrelevance, some to spiritual death. The New Age Movement is marketed to the public and many are buying. Note the proliferation of merchandise marketed as New Age jewelry, New Age music, New Age art and literature. Go to the bookstore and there you will find a growing section of New Age books. Like it's first century predecessors, the contemporary New Age Movement has an intense interest in all things coming from the East (Eastern Religion, particularly Zen Buddhism, Hinduism, and Taoism). In the United States, New Agers have added to these Eastern influences Native American spirituality. Mind you, none of these springs bubbling up in the American religious landscape is, in itself, as evil, unhealthy, or wrong. Rather, the Movement's lure is not to any one religion, but a hodgepodge of ideas borrowed here and there from both Eastern and Western religious traditions.

Frankly, if you believe Zen Buddhism is the way, the truth, and the life, then, by all means give your life to becoming a Zen master. If you find life and hope and meaning in Hinduism, then be a practicing Hindu. The same could be said for Judaism, Islam, Native American religion, or any of the world's religious systems. My concern is the subtle infiltration of my own tradition — Christianity — with ideas that, on the surface, look innocuous, but are in fact swirling undertows of confusion and ignorance.

So let's take a few minutes and explore four general characteristics concerning the New Age Movement and then look more carefully at Paul's Letter to the Colossians.[2] You may want to keep these in your mind as you are reading, experiencing and doing life, listening to music, reading literature, and/or viewing art in this particular moment of human history. These four general characteristics of the New Age Movement are key.

(1) *The New Age Movement is fundamentally reactionary.* By that I mean that it seems to have mounted a subtle assault on Western religion generally, and institutional Christianity specifically. The New Age Movement is a spiritual "resistance movement" against modernity, technology, the complexity of life, and the seeming impotence of the Christian church in this society. In a word, it offers individuals a spirituality that works. It sees a church that looks good on Sunday, but whose attendees leave and forget the faith they have celebrated in song and sermon. The New Age Movement is reacting against a Christianity it sees as, at best, present but impotent.

Do you see it? Within all of us, God created the need to experience reality in spiritual terms. God placed within us the desire to know God, to experience transcendence, otherness, and mystery; to ask questions, to stand in awe of creation and God's power. Unfortunately, in the grand sweep of modernity, the Christian faith has become rigid, even calcified: supremely rational, angular, and spiritually numb. Into this spiritual vacuum within our culture has come an intruder. The New Age Movement reacts to this rational, sterile, seemingly lifeless institutional Christianity by saying, "Become more introspective. Detach yourself from the complexity of life and the hypocrisy of western religion." Meaning? Move toward Eastern religion, move toward Native American spirituality, get back to Mother Earth. The New Age Movement is reactionary.

(2) *The New Age Movement is self-centered and tends to be self-serving.* It emphasizes meditation and self-awareness. Whereas my generation going through the 60s and 70s adopted the slogan "If it feels good, do it," the New Age Movement says, "If it feels good, believe it!" The New Age Movement talks about care for the earth, sensitivity to all living things, and so forth. It has an appearance of being outwardly focused, but down inside it is inwardly focused; it is an introspective, navel-gazing phenomenon that thrives on feelings. My spirituality — my peace — my feelings — me.

Now granted, the New Agers may find such inward peace and tranquility that their personal relationships are impacted for good. I have no quarrel with anyone genuinely seeking personal fulfillment, spiritual centeredness, or cosmic harmony. God knows, we could all use such hard-to-find realities.

Here's the problem: the New Age Movement holds out the carrot of harmony by playing to the instinct of self-fulfillment. Jesus, knowing well our fundamental human instinct for self-survival, turned such thinking on its head. Jesus said the urge to put me and mine at the center of one's spiritual quest is backwards. In fact, Jesus said, the only way to find one's self is to lose self in following him and serving others (see Matt 16:24-26 where Jesus confronted this self-saving attitude within the disciple band). Inward harmony is a wonderful goal. Jesus told us we cannot get there by first going inside. In fact, the Christian experience is first an outward journey of losing that leads in the end to finding. That journey, said Jesus, begins with the cross — an instrument of death not in the New Age vocabulary.

(3) *The New Age Movement is incredibly naive.* In a word, it does not take the whole issue of evil seriously. New Agers tend to look down at the realities of sin, evil, or Satan. The New Age Movement says, "Our problem is not sin, but ignorance. What you imagine as evil out there is not evil at all. Evil is our ignorance of what is really good." Here we find the subtle influence of Buddhism, which says, "I'm really not hurting, it's only in my mind." Pain is an illusion. Any of us that have had any pain know such thinking is baloney. Human pain and suffering are part of the human package.

Again, Jesus did not wink at human suffering. In fact, he took suffering so seriously, he endured our abandonment, disillusionment, hell and death, taking upon himself the pain of the world. Like it or not, human suffering and pain cannot and, I must say, should not, be imagined out of human experience. Though I would not choose suffering for myself or anyone I know, experience has taught me that life's depths cannot be fathomed without living through the experiences of suffering with faith. Victor Frankl taught us a lesson we still have difficulty accepting: though we do not always choose the circumstances of our lives, we always have the option of choosing our response to life's circumstances.[3]

A similar response can be leveled against the New Agers in terms of corporate evil and sin. Hitler was not misinformed about the Jews. His problem was not ignorance or illusion. Rather, Hitler was obsessed with self-preservation and self-aggrandizement. Racism in the United States was not and is not a problem of ignorance. Racism's roots are in self-security and self-love. Racism looks at "me" and judges all others on the basis of how "I" compare. The result: "I" become the measure of value. Others of differing color, nationality, religious or sexual orientation who do not stack up to "my" standard are inferior.

The Gospel does not trifle with or cozy up to sin: no illusion, no ignorance, no self-preserving mumbo-jumbo. Jesus looked sin square in the face. He took the reality of sin so seriously he died "for our sins" suffering in his body the no-exit experience of death. Sin is not rooted in illusion, indiscretion, ignorance, or poor judgment. Sin is rooted in our humanity; inextricably woven into the fabric of a life full of choices, the supreme choice being God or self. Mark it down, the New Age Movement is incredibly naive about suffering, evil and sin.

*(4) The New Age Movement is extremely deceptive and seductive.* It places overt emphasis upon spirituality, meditation, community, creativity, and harmony in all relationships. And all of that in and of itself is good. I'm not down on meditation, creativity, seeking harmonious relationships with others, or spirituality. Quite the opposite. The Christian faith champions all of these realities as gifts from God through which we experience God's presence and life. The New Age Movement, however, like its gnostic predecessors, has a way of window dressing its philosophy by emphasizing spirituality. Yet as we will see below from Paul's Colossian letter, the New Age Movement tends to distance itself from any personal relationship with Christ, awareness of Christ as Savior and Lord, and any understanding of God as Creator, Sustainer, Redeemer, and Friend. God is not so much personal as God, if "God" is used at all, is Life-Power. Seductively, the New Age Movement shifts the emphasis from what is important to what is trivial. And that subtle shift can grab you under the placid surface and sweep you in its undertow out to sea.

In summary, the New Age Movement — both ancient and contemporary — is reactionary, naive, self-serving, and deceptive. In my judgment, no one advocating New Age thought intends to convey any of these negative ideas. My hunch is that many individuals with Christian roots have bought into New Age concepts unaware of the undertow swirling under the movement's surface. Who would condemn any attempt to bring greater harmony and understanding to the human family? And yet, unknowingly, many Christian believers have embraced an idea and missed the larger message embodied in Jesus of Nazareth and the Gospel.

## Paul's Colossian Exposé

Paul's Letter to the Colossians is chock full of insight into the New Age phenomenon. As I alluded to earlier, the New Age Movement is actually an "old age" phenomenon. It is a sneaky old world philosophy that perhaps was more powerful and threatening in the first century than it is today. Believe me, the people who received the Letter to the Colossians were more threatened by the New Age Movement than we are. How so? In their day, New Age ideas had infiltrated so many religions — including Christianity and Judaism — and more than a few social institutions. The people to whom Paul wrote Colossians in the first century were being seduced and many taken out to sea by the undertow of this old world-New Age Movement. Paul, knowing the integrity of the Gospel was at stake, did not mince his words in addressing the dangers posed by the New Agers of the first century. Those same dangers lurk under the placid sea of the Christian church's situation today. Colossians 2:6-15 details Paul's indictment of the first century New Agers. His concerns can be summarized in three simple sentences.

**Jesus Christ is Lord of All**

Imprint two images in your mind. The first image is Jesus Christ is Lord. That's the theme of Colossians: Jesus Christ is Lord! We who have confessed Christ, received Christ by the work of the Spirit, and been baptized into Christ now live in Christ. Paul put it this way: "As you therefore have received Christ Jesus the Lord, continue to live your lives in him, rooted and built up in him and established in the faith, just as you were taught, abounding in thanksgiving" (Col. 2:6-7).

Now notice the number of times Paul speaks of being "in Christ," "in him," and "with him" in the verses that follow. Colossians 2:9, 10, 11, 12, and 13 contain one of these phrases no less than six times in five verses! On a larger scale, the "in Christ" theme is a predominant idea throughout Paul's letters.[4] In this particular letter, Paul is reminding the people that Jesus Christ is Lord. If you please, Paul insists the confession "Jesus Christ is Lord" forms a frame around all of life. No one can be Christian without living within the frame created by this simple but profound confession.

Several years ago our family spent six days in London. One of the many places we visited was the famous Tate Gallery, which houses one of the world's finest collections of paintings and sculptures. I remember the day well. We walked through its cavernous rooms viewing hundreds of paintings and sculptures. We saw works by Henri Matisse, Salvador Dali, Mary Cassatt, and others. The experience was memorable, awe-inspiring, exhausting.

I have a confession to make. Some of the paintings we saw in the Tate Gallery were not as engaging and memorable as the frames that held the paintings. Now I know that beauty is in the eye of the beholder. Many walk into the Tate Gallery and view a particular piece of art saying, "That is magnificent!" I look at the same work and ask, "What's that?" For me, viewing certain paintings is an exercise in amazement: I'm amazed "that" made it into "this" place! Truth to tell, many of the paintings I thought were less-than-awesome were held in a magnificent frame. For me, the frame was more elegant, more beautiful than the painting.

There is a frame that holds our lives in its elegant beauty. Paul says the frame around a believer's life is the confession, "Jesus Christ is Lord!" The Colossian philosophy was deceptively different. Many in the Colossian fellowship had changed "Jesus Christ is Lord" to "Jesus Christ and…." "Christ and gnostic-New Age philosophy," or "Christ and" something else. Paul insisted that "Christ *and*" anything is no substitute for "Christ *around*" everything. To use H. Richard Niebuhr's term, in his classic book *Christ and Culture*, Christ is the one "transforming culture." Christ around the reality that is my life. What frames your life? What words, what metaphors, what truths hold you in their grip? Paul says only one confession matters: "Jesus Christ is Lord!"

**The Undertow Is Always with Us**

Unlike the undertow at the beach that comes and goes depending on weather and surf conditions, this New Age undertow is always swirling under the surface in the shallow waters of contemporary life. Remember this: An unrecognized undertow is always active, challenging the confession of Jesus Christ as Lord. Paul told the Colossians: "You have the wrong picture in your frame." What did he mean?

Paul gave the Colossians three warnings as recorded in Colossians 2:8: "See to it that no one takes you captive by philosophy and empty deceit, according to human tradition, according to the elemental spirits of the universe, and not according to Christ."

(1) *This New Age spiritual undertow is invisible on the surface.* Write it down; life, by its nature, has a surf-pounding dimension to it. "Normal" life surf includes things like immorality, materialism, cynicism, or racism. Christian believers tend to recognize the dangers posed by "normal" surf issues. But here's the problem. The undertow, you'll remember, is invisible. It's underneath where the danger lies. In the strongest language Paul could use, he warns the church: "See to it no one takes you captive." The language suggests the taking of a city by stealth. The idea is simple: gnostic-New Age ideas will take you, unwittingly, out to sea. On the surface,

all looks well, even inviting. Paul's words are strong: "See to it, [watch out] that no one takes you captive."

What are the invisible, under-the-surface threats to contemporary Christian believers? What about the creeping influence of materialism, or the success syndrome, or "the latest craze" like the body beautiful, or technology's lure and fascination, or the never-ending career escalator, even a wholesome hobby can soon substitute for Christ. All these and many more look innocuous on the surface. Nevertheless, Paul warns that anything, anyone, or any philosophy that replaces God as the passion of our souls can sweep us out to sea and spiritual death.

How many folk have you known, perhaps you are one of them, who at one time took up a hobby only to discover the hobby taking up them? You name it. Golf became your passion; you wanted to play your best. That sounds innocent enough, doesn't it? But before long, golf became the hub around which your life revolved. Boating could be another example. After a while, you stopped owning a boat and the boat started owning you. You stopped having a place at the coast or the mountains; now the place has you. You stopped pursuing a career, as a means to provide for the needs of life. Now, the company–career–position has you.

This New Age undertow is invisible. Paul insists it is not "Christ and," it is "Christ around." The confession "Jesus Christ is Lord" is the only worthy frame around our lives. What belongs in the frame is not a career, a hobby, or even a person. What is rightfully framed by our confession of Christ is our lives. How quickly good things, good pursuits, good work, good anything can become the main thing. When we replace our lives–souls–selves framed by our Christian confession with any other thing, we discover, often after it's too late, that we have been swept out to sea by the invisible undertow of this age. Be careful. Good things can replace the Good One, even Jesus Christ.

(2) *This New Age undertow is a deceptive lie.* It's invisible on the surface and so deceptively alluring. The way this invisible undertow sweeps us out to sea is by what Paul calls, "hollow and deceptive philosophy." What is he saying?

Let's freeze time here. Suppose we could get in a time machine and return to the first century. In the city of Colossae, there in the Lycus Valley, in the western area of modern Turkey, there were three cities:

Hierapolis, Laodecia, and Colossae. All three of these cities came under the spell of a religious transformation beginning in the third century before Christ which endured to the third century after Christ. In that valley of opportunity, where traders came from Greece and went East and others came from the East and went West, much more than goods and money changed hands. There, the religions from the East met the religions from the West. A number of new religions were born mixing the mystery and awe of the East with the rationalism and structure of the West.

Over the span of many years, the people of this valley created new religions and changed old ones. Paul's phrase, "hollow and deceptive philosophy" needed little interpretation by the people who read this letter. They didn't have to say, "What's he talking about?" They knew exactly what he was talking about. What Paul was saying was obvious to the first readers of Colossians. "Just as that river valley had been a fertile field for the growing of new religions, you be careful, be very careful." One of the philosophies that surfaced in that era of time is what I have identified as Gnosticism. Mind you, there never was a "gnostic church," but Gnosticism, like today's New Age ideas, crept into Judaism and eventually into Christianity. Paul strongly tells it like it is: These fascinating and alluring ideas are a hollow and deceptive philosophy that says, "Christianity is okay but it is not quite enough." Jesus is okay, but so is Mohammed. Jesus is okay, but Buddha is good, too. The undertow is always with us; it never stops swirling under the shore of life. Be critically careful. Buddha and Mohammad, even Shirley MacLaine may offer more than a few insights into life. Even so, they are not Jesus Christ.

In our quest to be inclusive and politically correct, we are tempted to diminish our passion for Jesus Christ in an attempt to appease the voices of others. From time to time people ask me, "Pastor, I noticed this book in the bookstore. Is this a good book? Isn't this a New Age writer?" Some very fine thinkers–authors–guides of our day, like M. Scott Peck, Thomas More, and others have been labeled New Agers. Let me be clear: I am not saying they are or they are not, but what I'm saying is, read critically while reading as a believer whose confession is "Jesus Christ is Lord." Read Peck, read More, read widely and seriously, but read what you read with the frame "Jesus Christ is Lord" around your reading. Read good literature. Read the best thinkers of our time, but ask questions and consider the implications of what you read. "How does what this writer is saying inform my confession of Christ as Lord? Does what I'm reading impact life in Gospel terms? If so, how?" Ask questions with your confession of Christ as Lord around your reading. Paul still speaks: If we are not careful, a deceptive lie will sweep us away from relevance into the undertow of narcissism and selfishness. "Jesus Christ is Lord" must frame all of life.

(3) *This New Age undertow is not built on Christ.* Colossians 2:8c clearly indicates that gnostic-New Age thinking is, "Built on the human tradition and the basic principles of this world rather than on Christ." To use a construction metaphor, the foundation of all New Age thinking is human, earthly, temporal, and not on the person of Jesus Christ.

The old hymn we still love to sing says it best: "My hope is built on nothing less than Jesus blood and righteousness. On Christ the Solid Rock I stand…." If Jesus Christ is the frame around your life, you have nothing to fear from the New Age Movement. Absolutely nothing — zero! Why? Because you will discover New Age thinking is fundamentally shallow. Grains of truth are in it. Yes! Important and helpful insights into human nature and relationships are there within New Age thinking. What Christians can celebrate is that the healthy components of current New Age thinking can trace their origin not back to some self-appointed spiritual guru, but to Jesus Christ. Yes, many New Age writers and thinkers can help us understand and see areas where we may be blind, but as a system, New Age is hollow, deceptive, and theologically empty because it is not built on Christ.

**Community Calls Us in Christ**

Mark it down, this text does not say the world is evil. The text does not say the world is to be feared. The text does not say that the world is something from which we are to flee. What the text does say is this: Being "in Christ" radically changes the way we do life. The frame around our lives is the age-old confession "Jesus Christ is Lord." Saying Jesus Christ is Lord and having experienced Christ as Lord in our heart of hearts radically changes the way we live. Life's principles are not some motivational speaker's list of one-liners. Life's principles are to be Christ-centered — Christ-oriented — Christ-honoring.

The living Christ invites us to become filled with grace and forgiveness. Reconciliation is the way of the Christian life. To live in the confession of Christ as Lord is to open our arms and say, "I have been forgiven. I forgive and celebrate you as my brother and sister." Christian principles, by definition, include others in our circle of concern. God calls us to live a Christ-full vision of life that includes the community of faith, the Church. Such a call is not predicated upon sentences beginning with the words *Christ and*, but rather our calling celebrates the reality of *Christ around* all that is. Paul's masterful phrase is "Christ in you" which is another way of saying Christ around you and Christ transforming you.

What happens with devotees of the New Age Movement is predictably simple. Some Christian believers get so caught up in self improvement and every shifting wind that has the word "spirituality" associated with it. Before they realize it, they are swept away from their faith in Christ by the New Age undertow. This phenomenon happens in no small part because deep inside their lives, they are starving for authentic spirituality that is both intensely personal and significantly communal. Paul issues a warning. The Christian life is not a go-it-alone experience in which we find the prize at the deep end of our souls. Rather, the Christian life is deeply personal while simultaneously woven into a community of confessing brothers and sisters. We call that community the Church. Unfortunately, many churches today are losing more members to the undertow than they are retaining. The allure of a promised "deeper spirituality" without community accountability is hard to resist. The New Age Movement suggests one can find the ultimate spiritual experience solo. The New Testament says, "Not so!"

With unvarnished candor, the Bible tells the story of one who, having experienced Christian community, abandoned his spiritual friends for the unknown allure of something else. In the fourth chapter of Colossians, we meet a person Paul mentions with endearing language. In Colossians 4:14, Paul writes about two men who were friends. One man we know quite well because he wrote the third Gospel, the other is a new friend Paul introduces to us. Paul wrote, "Luke, the beloved physician, and Demas greet you." I don't really know who Demas was, but Demas was with Paul in prison at that moment of his life. We know Luke was a physician. Who was Demas? Was he a preacher? A lay leader? An elder? A deacon? We simply do not know. What we do know from Colossians is that Demas was so close to Paul, he was willing to be present with him even in prison. Such loyalty is commendable.

But when we read Paul's second letter to Timothy, we get another angle on Demas. Paul, years later, but still in prison, now writes these lines. Hear the pathos and pain in his soul as he writes to his protégé Timothy. "Do your best to come to me soon, for Demas, in love with this present world, has deserted me and gone to Thessalonica." I don't know who Demas was. But I know there was a moment when Christ was the frame, the confessional reality of his life, and yet something destructive happened; he fell in love with this world. To use our metaphor, the undertow swept him out into a rough sea away from Jesus Christ and the people of God.

If shallow relationships made with people who are primarily into their own journey is what you are really seeking, stay with the New Age crowd. If, however, you long for authentic spirituality in the company of people who, like yourself, know that at the deep end of their souls is something empty only God can fill, stay with the Church. Stay with the Christian community that, even in its broken moments, still confesses "Jesus Christ is Lord." Stay with Jesus' people who will call you to greater accountability, not less; greater service, not less; greater sacrifice and greater love.

In conclusion, if you have concern about the New Age Movement and, at the same time, your life is rooted in a personal relational with Jesus Christ, you have absolutely nothing to fear from the New Age section of the bookstore. Read all you choose to read by any New Ager you choose. Find out for yourself what they teach and then hold their "insights" up to the life and teachings of Jesus. While you are doing that, keep your life bonded to the community of faith and remember the Christian experience is corporate and sacrificial, not solo and narcissistic. If you still want to learn more about other journeys into the spiritual life, listen to people who are thinking out loud about how to do life, but do so with the confession "Jesus Christ is Lord" squarely around your heart.

Then, as opportunities arise, share what you are reading and hearing with other Christian believers. Listen as they tell you the story of their spiritual journey. Find community in a place where people are not afraid to read, question, search, wonder, and pray. And yes, if Christ is Lord, you will find life so enriching and full, you will discover a passion for life and for people. You will find yourself not only wanting to grow spiritually through personal meditation and prayer, not only concerned about the environment of our world, not only wanting to reconcile with other people, you will find yourself in love with God whose grace is radically transforming.

The New Age undertow still churns under the surface of the sea. Be careful. Place the confession of your faith in Jesus Christ around your life. Make Christ sole Lord of life and discover the great freedom to pray, serve, worship, and love following him. In so doing, you will engage life with courage and hope, free from the undertow sweeping so many out to sea.

## Prayer

God of all truth, source of every good and perfect gift, we are a confused and confusing people. We muddle through glib confessions of faith in Jesus Christ while arranging our lives as if he were only a footnoe to our life's story. Words tumble out of our often terrified hearts, stalked by the cynicism of this age, hobbled by our own well-managed hypocrisy.

Forgive us, we pray. Forgive us for presuming upon your grace while parading a piety that does not express our faith, much less reveal our hearts.

As you came in the midst of the storm to frightened disciples on an angry sea, so come to us this day. Speak to the terror within and show us through the ministry of your Spirit how empty is every tempting promise that does not find its life in you. Grant us discerning minds and sensitive imaginations to think your thoughts after you. So sharpen our senses that we will flee every form of shallow, casual confession of faith and in its place, engage our total selves in work and witness that is worthy of the One who gave his life for us, even Jesus Christ our Lord. Amen.

## Notes

[1]The gnostic Christian communities in northern Africa are the best examples we have of this phenomenon. See *The Nag Hammadi Library*, James M. Robinson, General Editor (San Francisco: Harper & Row, Publishers, 1977), for copious examples of Christian writing where gnostic thought captured orthodoxy.

[2] I am indebted to M. Scott Peck, M.D. *Further Along the Road Less Traveled* (New York: Simon & Schuster, 1993), 194-218, for much of the information in this synopsis.

[3] Victor Frankl, *Man's Search for Meaning* (New York: Pocket Books, 1963).

[4] See James S. Stewart's *A Man in Christ* (New York: Harper and Brothers Publishers, 1935) for the classic exposition of Paul's "in Christ" theology.

# The Danger of an Unholy Devotion

Therefore do not let anyone condemn you in matters of food and drink or of observing festivals, new moons, or sabbaths. These are only a shadow of what is to come, but the substance belongs to Christ. Do not let anyone disqualify you, insisting on self-abasement and worship of angels, dwelling on visions, puffed up without cause by a human way of thinking, and not holding fast to the head, from whom the whole body, nourished and held together by its ligaments and sinews, grows with a growth that is from God.

If with Christ you died to the elemental spirits of the universe, why do you live as if you still belonged to the world? Why do you submit to regulations, "Do not handle, Do not taste, Do not touch"? All these regulations refer to things that perish with use; they are simply human commands and teachings. These have indeed an appearance of wisdom in promoting self-imposed piety, humility, and severe treatment of the body, but they are of no value in checking self-indulgence. (Col 2:16-23)

In the last chapter, we talked about the undertow swirling beneath the surface of the New Age Movement. In cursory fashion, we examined the seductive ways in which the New Age Movement has infiltrated our culture in literature, art, music, and even religion. Remember too, that the New Age Movement is really not new at all: a great number of new age ideas were present in a first century philosophy called Gnosticism. When we study the religions active in the first century, we see gnostic-new age ideas bubble up and manifest themselves in Judaism, Christianity, and in many of the pagan religions of the ancient world. Today, we call it New Age. First century people did not know what to call it. Scholars refer to the first and subsequent centuries phenomenon as Gnosticism.

So the New Age Movement is not really new at all. It has been around a long time and will probably be with us always. It is incredibly seductive. It has a way of infiltrating established faiths like Judaism and Christianity with its teaching and values. On the outside, New Age looks innocuous, even appealing. But underneath the placid surface is a swirling undertow that can drown the Christian life in a shallow feel-good, self-centered spirituality.

Perhaps you are asking, how does New Age-gnostic thought infiltrate the lives of Christian believers? Put another way, is it possible for believers to be seduced unknowingly by New Age ideas? Sticking with Paul's letter to the Colossians, let's consider these questions under the heading of what I call the danger of an unholy devotion. As you read the following lines from Paul's ancient letter, forget for a moment that this was written in the first century and imagine it was written to us today. Notice how contemporary this text is, speaking to today's spiritual and behavioral concerns.

## Unholy Devotion

Paul does not mince his words. Clearly, the Colossians had a problem with letting go of their pre-Christian way of thinking in order to embrace fully the good news in Jesus Christ. In a word, Paul identifies the ways good things, even noble and worthy ideas, can become harmful, even destructive.

What is Paul getting at? Look more closely at the Colossian situation. Paul is writing to a group of Christian believers in the first century who confessed "Jesus Christ is Lord." Their lips' confession, however, was not hardwired to their lifestyle in a pagan, materialistic culture. Like many believers today, the ancient Colossian Christians were trying to merge their confession of Christ as Lord with a lifestyle alien to Christ. For them, it was Jesus *and* a number of other ideas and lifestyle expressions. Sadly, this "Jesus *and*" lifestyle has not changed in two thousand years. Today, confessing "Jesus Christ is Lord" is fraught with all kinds of confusions and dangers. Anyone who has followed Jesus very long or far knows how tempting it is to augment simple faith in Christ with alternative philosophies, lifestyles, and regulations.

Perhaps two stories from my life will help shed light on our dilemma. At fifteen years of age, in the simple concrete baptistry of the old First Baptist Church of Hialeah, Florida, with the loving help of my pastor Dr. Ernest R. Campbell, I was baptized in the name of the Father, the Son, and the Holy Spirit. In all candor, over thirty years later, I am still trying to understand what that meant and means. Like the church reformer Martin Luther, I find myself often looking in the mirror, needing to remind myself "I am baptized, I am baptized." An event took place "back there" out of which I am still finding strength and life here.

Another example: On July 12, 1975, Kathleen Lynn Pignato and I promised to love and cherish each other "till death parts us." I remember the moment well. Several hundred people witnessed the promises we made before Dr. Thomas Smothers in the beauty of First Baptist Church, West Palm Beach, Florida. Now, more than 26 years and three children later, both of us are still working on fulfilling that promise made to each other.

All of us have similar experiences. We speak a promise, we receive a blessing, we confess a faith only to discover it takes years, if not an entire lifetime, to find our lives, dreams, faith in the embrace of simple but profound words. In terms of our commitment to Jesus Christ, believers are constantly trying to understand what it means to live the confession, *Jesus Christ is Lord*. At times, we know success, blessing, joy in the arms of that confession. Who would question the spontaneous, soulful delight that shatters a long season of doubt when someone who is brother or sister prays with us or listens lovingly as we unwind the most painful of stories. And when the tale is told and the bleak darkness of despair is held between two believers, God's Spirit comes and brings a lifting of the burden; new joy breaks into both lives — the struggler and the friend. In that holy moment, two believers celebrate Christ's Lordship within, not apart from, life's changing circumstances. Dare we say that "for the rest of our lives" we are finding ways to express our baptismal confession?

But such remembering and thoughtful believing is not always a part of the story, is it? What can happen and what in fact did happen at Colossae — and is happening in all lives some of the time and some lives all of the time — is the blurring of our confession of and devotion to Christ as Lord. It is not that we do not love the Lord or that we intentionally forget Jesus. Rather, we embrace lifestyle choices and pick up "extra" spiritual baggage that dilutes our confession of Jesus as Lord of life. Rather than Jesus being the Lord of our lives, we relegate him as an "add on" feature, much like we would decide to add a CD player to our new car. We live "as if" Jesus can be tacked on to our well-managed lives and all will be well.

In this text from Colossians, Paul confronts this "Jesus *and*" attitude that is so pervasive among Christians and Christian communities. Allow me to paraphrase Paul's warning: *"Look out! Unholy devotions to provocative ideas may look okay on the surface, but in fact, they are deadly. Don't drown in the shallow water of such thinking."* Specifically, Paul mentions *two* lurking dangers that add nothing to our Christian faith.

**Rigid Religion**

The first one is what I call the danger of an unholy devotion to "rigid religion." Paul writes to people at Colossae who were all caught up in a "do not eat, do not drink, do not do this and that" kind of life. Read the text again — read it out loud for the full effect. At points, it sounds like someone talking to a two year old. Was Paul using such hand-slapping language because in fact, the Colossians were spiritual infants?

Rigid religion is dangerous stuff. At its core, it is judgmental, a religion of "do not's." Religion so defined ends up at a place called negativism. If you build your faith on what you cannot do, cannot say, cannot eat, cannot wear, cannot believe, or cannot think, you soon discover life is defined as a "do not" and "cannot" experience. Rigid religion cannot help being judgmental. Why? Because the person in the judge's seat has placed the rest of humanity into neat negative categories. Show me a person smitten by rigid religion and I'll show you a person whose life-perspective is fundamentally negative.

Not surprisingly, judgmental rigid religion is also fundamentally worldly. Surprised? Rigid religion suggests that the keeping of religious principles and the doing of religious things makes one right with God. Paul, the great champion of faith alone as our basis for being right with God, says emphatically "NO! Not so!" Many, particularly in evangelical, conservative homes, grew up with parents or grandparents who said,

"Good Christians don't play cards, don't go to movie houses, don't dance, don't smoke, don't chew, and don't hang around with those who do." The "doing" of any number of things off a list of forbidden behaviors marks you as being less than a Christian, if a Christian at all. Good Christians *don't*. When I think about that seriously, I must conclude that such a way of doing life is extremely worldly. It defines our relationship to God by what we don't do, rather than by who we are.

Do not miss it. Rigid religion is dangerous because it suggests — oh so carefully — that if you get your religion right, your behavior right, your actions right, then, you have got God right. God is right where you want God to be: on your side. Doing all the religious things "right" and not doing a whole list of other things that have nothing to do with grace, faith, or salvation, makes you "right" with God. There is a word for that kind of thinking: baloney! How easy it is in our lives to have an unholy devotion to those aspects of life God designed to be holy and good. Religion and religious devotion is surely one of them.

Islam, the great missionary religion that is captivating whole segments of our globe today, is a religion that is fundamentally "this worldly." Islam is also extremely rigid. Islam is logically precise, ritually exacting, behaviorally conforming, and notably intolerant. It is a "do this–do that" religion. Insisting on strict monotheism — with which both Jews and Christians agree — Islam nevertheless sees absolute obedience to Allah as the only way to achieve salvation. In fact, the word "Islam" means submission. Another way of thinking of Islam is to remember that those practicing the faith literally hug the earth during prayers.

This earth-hugging phenomenon is perhaps typified in the architecture of a mosque. Visit any of the large mosques in the Middle East and you will "feel" this aspect of their religion. The larger Muslim mosques are cavernous and spacious. Many of them are ostensibly beautiful. When you go into a mosque, however, no matter how high the ceilings, no matter how cavernous the room, you have the feeling that you must get down on the carpet. The room seems to pull you down to earth. The proper physical posture of a worshiping Muslim conveys this absolute obedience and subservience to Allah.

This same earth hugging phenomenon permeates the Christian faith in every outward expression of an inward spiritual and theological rigidity. Defining the gospel of freedom by creating a slavery to a list of absolute behavioral and spiritual norms is foreign to grace and unknown to Christ. Yes, Christian faith does result in a changed life. Yes, one cannot live in immorality, selfishness, greed, or brutality and pass as a Christian brother or sister. The Gospel, however, announces good news that grace pulls us in the direction of freedom to a higher obedience, not toward the bondage of rules.

Believers are called to live out of faith, not from a list of rules. How easy it is for us in the Christian family to develop an unholy devotion to rigid religion that becomes judgmental, negative, and proscriptive. Paul says, "Be careful." We in the church must take this to heart. If we are not careful, we will teach our young people that Christianity has everything to do with observing religious rituals and obeying religious rules. We can too easily communicate the ridiculous notion that "good Christians" are those who go to church, be good (whatever that means), and live a boring life. A religion it may be, but it is not Christianity.

If you define your Christianity by some rigid set of things you don't do, you may have found something, but you have not found the faith for which Jesus died and rose again. And yet, we have unwittingly communicated to those within and without the Christian family that "the faith once for all delivered to the saints" is actually "the rules once for all required of the saints." If you get the religion right, so the argument goes, you are right, orthodox, accepted, righteous. Where is faith? Where is grace? Where is Jesus Christ's "once for all" sacrifice on the cross to free us from our sins? Paul says, "Be careful about this unholy devotion to rigid religion."

## Puffed–Up Piety

Paul then notes a second unholy devotion that can creep into our lives: puffed-up piety. Listen again to Paul's warning. "Do not let anyone who delights in false humility and the worship of angels disqualify you for the prize. Such a person goes into great detail about what he has seen and his unspiritual mind puffs him up with idle notions." Puffed-up piety too soon becomes an unholy devotion to that which is not of Christ.

Lest we think this phenomenon died in the first century never to infect the Christian family again, think again. Puffed-up piety suggests that certain people and certain behaviors enable you to experience a closer relationship to God than other people or behaviors. If you can be like "the pious ones," you can be closer to God. A person smitten with puffed-up piety brags about the volume of their Bible reading and the hours they spend in prayer. Puffed-up piety says, "I've got the correct theology. Not only have I read a lot of Bible and prayed a lot of prayers, and have the right theology, but the rest of you are all wrong. If you could just be as spiritual as I am." Paul sounds a warning. This kind of puffed-up piety — this kind of peacock-strutting religion — is not of Christ.

Anytime you and I get to the place in our lives where we think we've got all the answers, believing our way of living the Christian life is *the* way and everybody else is less Christian, we have missed the message of Jesus Christ. Do not misunderstand me. There is nothing wrong with — in fact, there is much very *right* with — reading your Bible daily and finding a place to pray privately. All of us are wise to work very carefully in the Scriptures to understand what God is saying and to work out our own theology under the Spirit's leadership. All of that is healthy, wholesome, even necessary. But if we ever get to the place where we think that our Bible reading, praying, and theology is *the* meaning of Christianity, we have missed the message and the Lord who gave his life for us.

Paul deftly insists that anyone can develop an unholy devotion to a rigid religion of rules and regulations or be so caught up in narrowly defining your faith as *the* faith, that your supreme devotion to Jesus Christ takes second fiddle.

Practically speaking, both of these unholy devotions lead to a Christless Christianity. How so? Because one's devotion to rigid religious rules or ostentatious, self-centered piety take our lives away from Jesus Christ, who alone is the rightful Lord. Forcefully, Paul said people who are caught up in rigid religion and puffed up piety are out of touch with Jesus Christ and are "at risk" spiritually. This self-measured spirituality is a distorted vision of the Christian mission and message.

**Finding Holy Devotion**

Now that we have caught a glimpse of the problem, what are some ways we can grow in holy devotion to Jesus Christ? To paraphrase Paul's words, the Christian faith is really not about angels or one's comprehension of some fine point of theology, or even one's ability or inability to jump through a whole sequence of ritual hoops. Rather, Christian faith is all about a personal relationship with Jesus Christ in which Christ — not rules, theology, or feelings — is changing us into his image. Is this not what Paul had in mind when he wrote "As you therefore received Christ Jesus the Lord, continue to life your lives in him" (Col 2:6)? That is Christianity. And yet how easy it is for us to find ourselves devoted to, almost possessed by and obsessed with, all kinds of other things.

Paul says that if we have not framed our lives with Jesus Christ, if Jesus Christ is not Lord of life and we are not in relationship with him, we are in danger of drowning in the shallow waters of unholy devotions. Here is a pointed word to those of us within the organized, institutional church at the dawn of the twenty-first century. His caution is simply this: If we are not careful, our love for Christ's Body, the Church, will devolve into an unholy devotion to the institution rather than to the Head of the Church, who is Jesus Christ. Institutions are important and the institutional church is a viable dynamic entity in many of our lives. Church is an important, sustaining reality for so many of us born and bred under the shadow of a steeple somewhere. But our love for the institutional church cannot now or ever be our life's devotion. Our life's devotion must be to the person of Christ and him alone. He is the head and only Lord of the Church visible and invisible. Our primary loyalty is to Christ.

To take this a bit further, those of us within the Church rightfully have a love for high ethics and morality, orderly, dignified worship, the correct use of language, and accurate theological reasoning. All of these wholesome ideals, however, can seductively drown us in good things, and yet miss the person of Jesus. Do not misunderstand what Paul is saying. It is important that Christians live upholding high ethical standards and high moral principles. It is imperative that when we worship God we do so thoughtfully, reverently, and with dignity. Worship must be God-centered. It is important that we work on developing a theology that awakens faith to its relational responsibilities. All of these noble goals surely strengthen God's Church. But . . . they cannot sustain the heart's devotion. Our heart's devotion is to a person, and that person is the Lord Jesus Christ.

So how do we find a holy devotion to Jesus Christ, lest we drown in religion's shallow water? Paul offers some helps from his own experience.

**Live as free as Christ made you**

During my college years, the founder of our college and my preaching professor was Dr. Jess Moody. Dr. Moody is a wonderful person. As he was lecturing one day he said, "Fellas [there were no women in my preaching class in 1973], if you ever get to the place where you don't hear the trumpets in the morning, you ought to pack it up and walk away from the ministry. You are called of God. Wake up in the morning and hear God's trumpets summoning you to your work." Not too long ago, after two hours of sleep, I woke up trying to hear trumpets, but all I could hear were tubas! I know what Dr. Moody was saying, however: Our calling should summon us to God's work.

Read again the following verses from Colossians and, as you do, listen to the call to freedom Paul gave those first century believers. Paul put the trumpet to his mouth and said, "Live free in Christ!"

> Since then you have been raised with Christ, set your hearts on things above, where Christ is seated at the right hand of God. Set your minds on things above, not on earthly things. For you died, and your life is now hidden with Christ in God. When Christ, who is your life, appear, then you also will appear with him in glory. (Col 3:1-4)

What is Paul saying? At the very least, he is reminding us that our lives find uncommon joy and exhilarating passion when we discover God has made us to be free persons in Christ! None of us need walk around with our past and the burdens of life weighing us down and crushing us under its load. Add a list of religious regulations on top of that and faith becomes a burden, not a delight. Paul says, "No! You have been created in Christ to be free." Live free, for your life has died and you have been raised with Christ.

Anyone who was alive at that moment of moments when communism collapsed under its own oppressive weight, will remember the exhilaration and spontaneous joy bubbling out of the lives of persons living then behind the Berlin Wall. When the Soviet Union fell apart, that "Wall of Death" was opened and Berliners and Germans from everywhere came and jumped on that wall and celebrated the fall of communism and the opening of their society to freedom and democracy. One of the pictures I have in my mind of that moment is of men and women, boys and girls, jumping up on that wall with chisels and hammers in their hands literally beating the wall into the dust of history. Why? Because now they were free.

Would somebody in the Christian family please tell me why believers in Jesus Christ who have been redeemed through his death, saved by his life, and made free by the grace of God, spend time building walls around life rather than tearing them down? Live free. Do not build walls around yourself or others. Refuse to build any kind of wall: walls of rules, religious walls, ritual walls, theological walls, gender walls, class walls, denominational walls. The Gospel declares we are free. Live free under the Lordship of Christ.

**Major on majors and minor on minors**

Paul throws down the gauntlet. I can almost hear him say, "My dear Colossian brothers and sisters, please, for God's sake, be a 'big picture' Christian." Some Christians, God bless them, are obsessed with the faith's trivialities; minor textual, theological, and ritual issues that matter to no one outside the faith and few inside. The old question, both laughable and embarrassing is, "How many angels can dance on the head of a pin?" Now, other "major" questions come to the shallow surface: "What about the seventh head of the beast in the thirteenth chapter of the Book of Revelation?" That's real important to some folks. Paul begs us, "Be a big picture Christian." Christ-less Christianity has an unholy devotion to unimportant theological trivia.

Truth to tell, any of us may find any number of biblical, theological, and philosophical issues piquing our curiosity. They may offer an interesting pursuit intellectually, but do not sell your soul to them. Major on the majors. Be a big picture Christian. The big picture of Christianity is grace and forgiveness, reconciliation and service, living through life's scrapes and battles with a God-given sense of purpose born of Christ.

Talk about finding holy devotion, how can we if the main thing in our lives spiritually is some sidebar issue that does not ultimately matter. Thinking Christians must take this to heart and find freedom in Christ from the trivial pursuits so many believers find intoxicating. To be a Christian believer in the 21$^{st}$ century requires us to communicate the big picture where we work, were we play, where we shop, wherever we engage others in relationships. It is a scathing indictment on the Christian family to consider how many nonbelievers have only viewed the "unholy devotions" of practicing Christians. When we get the big picture out of focus everything else falls apart. Be a big picture Christian.

**Lead Jesus-Centered Lives**

In Colossae, people's concerns with angels and calendars and visions and moons and foods and rituals was much the same problem we face today. All we've done is change the focus a bit. I know some people today who are so infected with the angel phenomenon that you can hardly have a conversation with them without talking about angels. "Have you read this book on angels?" "Have you heard this speaker on angels?" "Did you see that television program on angels?" It's angels, angels, everywhere! Angels have become the passion of so many lives. Angel pins, angel jewelry, angels books, and angel sightings are the rage of millions of Americans. When you think about the whole craze — it is crazy! — you have to consider the fact that in the past five years, there have been more angel sightings and hype than in the first 20 centuries of the Christian faith.

What's going on? Some believers in the Christian movement have been, are, and always will be, absolutely consumed with the particular theological issue of the day. That "thing" becomes the passion of their hearts. In one era it is the millennium, in another Satan, and another the gifts of the Spirit. Today, it is angels. For Paul, the only worthy center of his life was the crucified and risen Lord. To the Corinthians, Paul insisted Christ crucified and risen was the folly and foundation of the faith. To these Colossians, Paul declared, "Christ in you, the hope of glory"(Col 1:27).

These unholy devotions all too easily slip into our everyday lives in an unholy, unhealthy way. Any time you and I are more concerned about the weather on the weekend than we are about the worship of God, we might want to look at our devotions. Some today are more concerned about being politically correct and connected than they are about being spiritually alive. Truth to tell, we can become so obsessed by the minor, sidetrack issues of life that we miss all the joy of living in the big picture of the grace, mercy, and love of God. Again, major on majors — minor on minors.

**Celebrate relationships and value people**

Our supreme example is Jesus. Jesus always majored on relationships with people because he valued each person as uniquely created in the image of God. Putting your life's exclamation points on Jesus and others will inoculate you from giving your life to any unholy devotion. These unholy devotions, minor things, become the passion of life. When we give ourselves to these unholy devotions, we get all caught up in our little particular theme or theology or issue and Jesus and people get left behind. We find ourselves so wrapped up in presenting our point of view or debating and winning some point of theology, needing to walk away victorious, we end up only wrapped up in ourselves. And for what? Who do we leave behind? We leave people and we leave Jesus. We sacrifice our Gospel birthright — which is all about relationships — for a list of theologies, ideas, and clichés that aren't worthy of our life's devotion.

I know people in the community where I live — you know them where you live — who would absolutely run you over getting to a bookstore to buy the latest book on angels, but who would not go across town to deliver clothes to a needy family. I know folk in our community who would move heaven and earth to be politically connected, correct, and rightly postured who seem to give little or no energy to being spiritually dynamic and vital. Such are the dangers of an unholy devotion.

Put simply, unholy devotions become substitutes for Jesus. Frame your life with Jesus Christ. Give your heart's passion to Jesus Christ. Do so, and you will be more like Jesus in whose image God longs to make you. You will become the full, redeemed human being God calls you to be following Jesus Christ. Be careful. Make Jesus your heart's passion. All unholy devotions are less than worthy of your time, your dreams, your energy, your all.

# Prayer

There are times, our Father, when we settle for the good rather than reaching for the best. We who are told by a hungry economy that we are only consumers, long for transforming life that only you can give. Forgive us for filling the empty but greedy pockets of our souls with phoney substitutes for you. Grant us the courage to see others, even ourselves, as persons who need no simple formula for shallow living, but rather a life-changing relationship with you.

Summon us, we pray, to a holy devotion to you. Re-create us in Jesus Christ to love the things you love, to flee from every form of inhumanity and greed, to welcome you in our lives as the one who transforms night into day, who brings life from death.

God of generous love, so fill us with your higher purposes in Christ that we will submit ourselves only and always to you, for you alone are worthy. Through Jesus our Lord we pray. Amen.

# The Beached Family

Wives, submit to your husbands, as is fitting in the Lord. Husbands, love your wives and do not be harsh with them. Children, obey your parents in everything, for this pleases the Lord. Fathers do not embitter your children, or they will become discouraged. Slaves, obey your earthly masters in everything; and do it, not only when their eye is on you and to win their favor, but with sincerity of heart and reverence for the Lord. Whatever you do, work at it with all your heart, as working for the Lord, not for men, since you know that you will receive an inheritance from the Lord as a reward. It is the Lord Christ you are serving. Anyone who does wrong will be repaid for his wrong, and there is no favoritism. Masters, provide your slaves with what is right and fair, because you know that you also have a Master in heaven. (Col 3:18–4:1)

It is 5:30 a.m., any Tuesday, when the alarm wakes a near comatose Mom from deep sleep. Dad wiggles his eyebrows knowing he's got to move from the horizontal to the vertical as soon as his bride of 8 years leaves the ceramic "throne" to go downstairs to the kitchen. The kids — Tyler and Melanie (4 years old and 18 months) — are still sleeping (thank God!). While Mom throws together a quick breakfast, Dad shaves and jumps in the shower. It's now 5:45 a.m., his shower over and breakfast looking reasonably together, they trade places. He moves down the hall to awaken the little ones which — Dad loves this — includes changing Melanie's diaper and making sure Tyler makes it to the toilet. Dad and the two cubs go downstairs where they eat breakfast. Mom is doing her thing in the shower, followed by the hair dryer, makeup routine, etc.

It is now 6:04. Dad has presided over juice and cereal and now, throwing what can be washed in the dishwasher and everything else in the garbage, tries to corral Tyler and Melanie upstairs where he dresses them — not an automatic "easy" for any male — before plopping them down before the morning cartoon show that will somehow pacify the kids till he and Mom finish getting ready. Fast forward. At 6:55, Tyler and Melanie are unloaded at a daycare facility between their home and the parents' jobs. Today, Dad drops them off because on Tuesdays, Mom has an executive leadership breakfast with senior management at 7:00 (she has the drop-off duty the other four mornings because daycare is in the direction of her office).

Fast forward more. It is now 5:48 p.m. Mom picks Tyler and Melanie up from daycare, cruises through the drive-in window of the local fried chicken, instant dinner place, makes three calls on her cell phone while managing of all this (the pediatrician — Tyler has a fever, her husband's cell number — which is busy, and a friend who is supposed to drive the soccer car pool that evening), and manages to "relate" to her two children while moving in at least three directions. Exhausted? I am.

I could go on, but you know the drill. The family today is hurried, tired, pressed, over-scheduled and under-nurtured. This scene between home–daycare–work–fast food–sports teams–church and countless other places is more common than any of us care to admit. We are moving at wimped-out light speed into the third millennium wringing our hands about the demise of the traditional family tree while swinging an axe at its trunk. What gives?

In a word, the family may be the shallowest of institutional relationships in contemporary American life. Even in young families — often those without children — the two career time crunch, get–ahead–before–its–too–late lifestyle crowds out times for conversation, problem solving, and intimacy. Maturing families, where children's schedules are as busy as the parents, find even eating a meal together to be an effort filled with frustration. I shutter to think how many missed opportunities for deepening family ties litter American society because parents want "only the best" for their children (the best soccer team, the best piano lessons, and so forth). Sad to say, families are drowning in the shallow waters of the promised good life that never happens. The anticipated "golden years" when couples can enjoy each other, their adult children and grandchildren too many times become the shuttle years, as parents now divorced must navigate not one or two sets of in-laws, but also the blended family's children and in-laws. The relationships can get complicated. More times than not, these meandering family connections become increasingly shallow, brief, and conflicted.

Single parents fare no better. Not long ago, we were traveling in another city when we stopped at a fast food restaurant to catch a quick supper. As we looked around the room, we noticed table after table occupied by a single mom or dad with his or her child or children. The time was 6:00 p.m. or so. We could only imagine what the last hour had been like. The day done, these mothers and fathers battled crawling traffic to the suburbs, picked up their young from daycare at 5:45 and were now eating supper before going home, having perhaps a few minutes of "quality" time; then baths, bedtime rituals, and sleep. Guess what? These hurried adults and children rise tomorrow and do it all over again.

Where are the opportunities to create "home?" How do adults expect their children to have memories of meaningful table talk, family storytelling, value transmission, even spiritual–religious conversations in such an environment? To take any time at all running similar family scenarios through your mind is to end up at a place called despair, or worse, death. From the stories I have heard in my pastoral work, the above experiences are not uncommon in contemporary American life. Is there a way to rescue the American family?

Before we can attempt to answer that question, let's get the problem focused. You know the situation. Young adults marry for "love" only to discover that marriage and family require another definition of love undiscovered in the heat of premarital romance. What is required of a man and a woman who enter the sacred covenant of marriage? and, Why is this most sacred and happy bond subject to such brutality and torture at the hands of the very people who pledged to "love and cherish" each other "'til death parts us"? What gives?

Best-selling author Dr. Kevin Leman said in a 1999 lecture at First Baptist Church of Augusta that the typical marriage moves along a near-predictable path from expectations to reality to disillusionment. A couple marries with a high set of expectations of their mate and marriage. Not long after the credit card bills are paid from the honeymoon, reality sets in. The months pass into a few years when little–changing reality leads to disillusionment. Unless this downward spiral stops, disillusionment becomes license to be unfaithful which soon leads to separation or divorce. How does newlywed joy devolve into such disaster?

The beach can give us some help. From time to time along the eastern coast of the United States, a whale will beach itself to the horror and eventual frustration of us helpless human beings. I have always been fascinated as to why whales beach themselves. As many of you know, pilot whales even beach themselves in groups; the whole herd swims to shore and to death. Why? Put simply, the group's leader gets disoriented and loses his way. Other times, single whales end up on the beach, unable to find their way back to deeper water. How does this happen? Is it inevitable that these magnificent creatures — the largest on earth — must suffer such a fate in the very water that sustains their lives?

The reason whales beach themselves is a lingering mystery to marine biologists. Theories abound. The most believable — at least to me — suggests that a tiny parasite lodges itself inside the whale's inner ear or brain. As that parasite moves into the whale's auditory system and/or the brain, the whale loses the ability to echolocate; meaning, to use his or her internal navigational sonar. With the parasite in the ear or the brain, the whale loses its ability to know whether or not it is in shallow water or deep water. Sadly, the whale cannot locate itself in the very environment that can sustain its life: deep water.

And so, a victim of what we would call vertigo, the whale becomes disoriented, ending up on the beach and death. Know this for certain: the whale does not choose to die. Rather, the presence of an unknown and sinister intruder short-circuits the whale's natural, God-given directional equipment. The "something" that has lodged inside its body is foreign and unwanted. The whale doesn't know it is there, much less how to get rid of it.

I wonder if such a phenomenon is occurring in marriages and families all across our nation. Could it be that husbands and wives, moms and dads, even sons and daughters, have been invaded by a parasite that is slowly dismembering the family's God-given navigational equipment? Consider current data. Facts available about family today in the media and on the information super-highway are legion. We are collecting more data about families today than perhaps any subject in our society. Why? Because we have a fascination with family. Specifically, social science professionals are concerned as to why so many American families are dysfunctional, broken, and hurting. So scientists, sociologists, psychologists, and researchers of all kinds gather data about family like bees gather pollen. And there is much data to gather.

## The Facts

Consider the following four facts about American families I found both provocative and disturbing:

*Fact number one.* According to the Census Bureau, one out of four American children is growing up in a single-parent household. That's 18 million children.[1] Forget the spiritual–moral–covenantal aspects of marriage for just a moment. 18 million children in single parent families is a major concern to any government responsible for the welfare of human beings under 18. We're talking money — lots of money — expended by federal, state, and local governments for indigent medical treatment, childcare, food stamps, and so forth. To be sure, not every single-parent family is on public assistance, but responsibility for the welfare of children is shared by the government and parents. Thinking people have other concerns. The beached family in the United States, like the beached whale, is an enormous waste of resources both physical and spiritual. A psychiatrist friend reminded me not long ago that God's design for rearing children requires a mother and a father. Children need both parents. Two parents complement each other. Where one parent tends to be indulgent ("You want it, you can have it!"), the other parent holds back ("No, you'll have to wait until your next birthday before we'll consider letting you have an electronic game like that.). Such balance teaches the child invaluable lessons about relationships, resources, stewardship, responsibility, and delayed gratification. I have great respect for single parents. Single parenthood, however, is not God's design for rearing children.[2]

*Fact number two.* On any given night, four out of every ten children in America will be sleeping in a house in which their father does not live.

That is 10.5 million children who go to sleep without a father in the home to read them a story, tuck them in, and protect them from danger. For children born in the 1990s, this number will likely rise to six out of every ten.[3]

Stop right now. Get that thought out of your mind. I am not down on mothers. Being a dad, however, requires me to think about the implications of children whose fathers have abandoned them or deliberately checked out of their lives. Thinking women know that God's design for rearing children not only requires two parents, but needs the firm and faithful hand of a caring, devoted, involved man known to his children as "Dad."

How strong is a Dad's influence on a child? You tell me. Tell me who can substitute in a nine-year-old girl's life for her father? Who can be to her that non-manipulative, appropriately touching, strong armed, spiritually guiding presence other than her father? Tell me, who can teach a ten-year-old boy that it is okay to cry when you hurt; that real men not only do cry, but real men must cry to discover their full humanity and masculinity? Tell me, who can teach boys and girls the problem-solving skills hard-wired into males; skills that must be balanced by problem-coping skills woven into the fabric of being a woman? I don't know about you, but I'm not proud of the fact over 10 million boys and girls go to bed each night in America without their father's presence in the house they call home.[4]

*Fact number three.* The book *Sex in America* reports that 20% of women and as many as 35% of men have been unfaithful to their spouses. *Christianity Today* did a survey among its subscribers — mostly evangelical, conservative Christians — and found that 23% of their readers had engaged in extramarital sex![5] It gives me no joy to announce that fornication and adultery are alive and well in the conservative, Bible-believing population of the United States. All of us know the truth. Human beings are sexual their entire lives. We are, by God-given design, a sensual, feeling, touching, kissing, relating, orgasmic species. Our sexuality is not a part of our being; sexuality is much of the essence of our being.

Simply put, human beings are so sexually oriented that God instituted a bold covenant in which we could, with God's blessing, experience and enjoy the full range of our sexuality. Marriage is that institution.

Marriage is God's gift to a man and a woman who promise to live faithfully before and with each other all the days of their lives. Marriage is not a game, an experiment, a "season of love," a "thing," or an arrangement. Marriage is God's gift in relationship to a couple in whose lives God is present and recognized.

From time to time, I have wondered what crosses a man or a woman's mind after the thought of adultery plays games with the head. Yes, I am as sexual as you are and yes, the adultery thought has crossed my mind as it has every man and woman who has ever lived. The curious thing for me, at least, is what crosses the mind next? Put another way, what *fails* to cross the mind next?

For example, does it ever occur to a man being pursued by another woman that, having "captured" you, she will no doubt, in time, go pursuing other men? Does it occur to a woman being chased by a man who is either single or married, that, having savored the spoils of conquest, he will, given time, go hunting once again? The facts are clear: people who cannot remain faithful to their promises live lives of duplicity and dishonesty. Sexual conquest is another feat in a long list of challenges presented to a man or a woman. Unfaithfulness is an act of selfishness, pleasure without commitment, and spiritual contempt. Hollywood has glamorized it, the soap operas have institutionalized it, short-sighted adults have dabbled in it, and all of us are suffering the consequences of it. In a word, adultery is stupid.

Truth to tell, there is more to adultery than sex. That is right, there are more ways to commit adultery than simply engaging in sexual behavior with another person. One can commit adultery by abandoning a mate for a career, or children for a promotion. Many today are committing adultery by engaging in unbridled devotion to a college football program, a professional basketball team, or a golf handicap. Make no mistake about it, unfaithfulness to one's spouse and/or family may not be sexual at all. For many, sexual adultery has never been a temptation. Non-sexual adulterers are, however, so loyal to their team, university, career, hobby, you name it, that family is left alone and abandoned.

*Fact number four.* In a survey of four and five year olds, published by Reader's Digest (January 1995), 33% of them said they'd rather give up their fathers than television. Like fact number two, this troubling bit of information is a scathing indictment of men in America. That's right, men, not television. If dads were investing time with their children, the television would often sit silent and untouched in the corner of the room. There is a double-edged sword here. We dads watch our share of television tacitly communicating what's important in the house is on the tube, not each other. We communicate by our actions that television and other forms of entertainment are superior to deep, meaningful relationships with those with whom we share family. The facts are in: television is winning while the family drowns in shallow water.

## Let's Go Further

As a Christian believer, I have a shameless bias. I understand family to mean "Christian" family. So, let me take a stab at defining the Christian family. The Christian family is one in which the family unit finds its spiritual strength and identity from a personal and meaningful relationship with Jesus Christ and seeks to live according to the teachings of Jesus. By family unit, I mean single families, traditional nuclear families, and blended families. However you define the family unit where you call home, a Christian family finds its spiritual strength and identity from a personal and meaningful relationship with Jesus Christ and seeks to live according to the teachings of Jesus. Let's put that definition to work.

Get in your time machine and come with me again to Colossae in the first century, to the little Christian church to which Paul wrote a letter. The Colossian believers had read nearly three-fourths of the letter when they got to Paul's teaching on marriage and family in the third chapter. German scholars have called this section of Paul's letter the *Haustafeln*, meaning, "the Housetables," or "Rules of the House." Ephesians 5 and 1 Peter 3 contain other examples of these "Housetables" in the New Testament. The Colossian housetables comprise the first century Christian family's responsibilities to each other. Make note, these verses do not cover every conceivable situation in family, but they do highlight the more important roles we fill in relationship to others within family. Some of the rules for this first century family are difficult to translate into contemporary life. Nevertheless, timeless principles apply that can help us today.

Notice first of all the configuration of the first century family. It sounds similar to and yet so unlike family today. The first century roles within family were: Wives, Husbands, Children, Slaves and Masters. Those last words — slaves and masters — leave us cold. Candidly, first century slavery was an accepted social institution by both Christians and non-Christians. That none of the writers of the New Testament, including Paul, condemned slavery is troubling to say the least. Most scholars believe Paul's understanding of slavery was as a nonviolent, nonabusive institution. Even so, slavery was and is an inhuman, destructive institution. At this point, let it be enough to remember that slavery was a part of first century life. We today decry any social system that denies full human rights to all human beings. Indeed, the human family cannot tolerate any discriminatory or dehumanizing behavior that insults human beings made in the image of God.

Having noted one of the textual ambiguities in the text, know for certain there are others. Quite honestly, I have a serious dilemma as I read these verses. I am overwhelmed by the fact that fully half of this entire text has to do with slaves and masters. Now I did not count the words, but you can look at the text yourself and see that more than half of this section is addressed to slaves and masters.

Why is that so? Why did Paul spend fully half of his space addressing slaves and masters? It seems to me there are a couple of possibilities. The first possibility is that slaves made up a large portion of the Colossian church. Paul knew the Colossian church had numbers of slaves in their membership. We know from church history that many of the early Christian believers were slaves. They brought the Christian faith into the homes where they served and no doubt shared their faith in Christ with their masters.

A second possibility is this: slaves had trouble — as they should have had trouble — with believing a faith (the Gospel) that announced their freedom in Christ, and yet was not apparently having any effect on their circumstances. It is one thing for preachers to talk about freedom in Christ. It is another thing, as we say, to face the reality where the water hits the wheel. I suspect that slaves in that congregation were having no small problem with reconciling the freedom announced in the Gospel — freedom from sin, death, and hell — and the fact they were still in physical bondage.

With those two possibilities in mind, we have no choice now but to become interpreters of this text. What do we do with it? If slavery is not an issue in our society — and we thank God that it is not, and we pray for the day when all the human family will be freed of that — then what do we do with these verses? How does the third millennium Christian family interpret these verses? Do we cut them out? Do we look the other way and say, "Let's give this passage a spiritual application?" Do you see our struggle as we wrestle with a text like this? Wait a second! Either we spiritualize Paul's teaching or we read these verses with interest and then rightfully decide that this is part of Paul's letter that is culturally oriented to the first century having no application today. Meaning? We put these verses in their first century context and almost ignore them because of their unique first century context.

At that moment, when you and I choose either of those two options, we become interpreters of the text, do we not? Honesty compels us to say, "That situation applied to the first century, but it does not apply today." Let me give you another example. In 1 Corinthians 11, Paul spends fourteen verses writing about the proper length of a man or a woman's hair. Can you believe that? Fourteen verses on hair! This was a big issue at Corinth. Paul clearly taught that women were to let their hair grow long and men were to keep their hair short. Women were not to shave their heads, but were to wear veils in church to keep the angels from desiring more intimate relationships with the Corinthian women. Sounds odd, does it not?

In most Christian churches, on any given Sunday morning in the United States, most women and not a few men are in violation of this text. Furthermore, Paul's teaching concerning the wearing of veils is ignored wholesale by women in the industrialized nations of the world. My point? When we wrestle with the text interpretively, we must make interpretive decisions based upon the culture of the first century over against the culture and perspective of the twentieth century. Every reader of the Bible wrestles with these kind of issues as an interpreter.

But once the right and necessity to interpret is granted, once we begin to do that and realize some of the Bible is oriented culturally to another century, then we have to make another decision. If interpretation is granted for understanding Paul's teaching on slaves and masters, we must also consider other parts of this text and ask, How do we interpret the whole? Does this text describe or picture the family in the 21st century? And if not, what is God's word to family today through this first century text?

With that in mind, let's press on with another question: Is this text primarily about our roles in the family? Or, is the text about relationships within the family? If the text is about roles, then wives must submit to husbands, husbands must love wives, children must obey parents, and fathers must not embitter their children. If the text is about roles within the family, this is the important issue within the text on which we must focus. If, however, this text is about relationships, we must ask another question. What does this text say about relationships in the family?

In my judgment, this is the more important question. Why? Because we can establish proper roles within family according to biblical principles and miss the more important responsibility of deepening relationships between members of the family. My experience tells me that many of the families around my life have the husband–wife–children–parents role down pat. They are, however, miserably lacking in deep and meaningful relationships between the husband and wife, children and parents. If the family is beached and suffocating on a lonely shore, shallow relationships may be the reason.

## Relationships Are Key

The Christian family today is struggling for its spiritual soul. The issue, in my judgment, is not role definition, it is relationships. We can spend all our time wrestling with role definition and miss relationships and, in missing relationships, miss the genius, the uniqueness, the depth of the Christian family. What makes your family Christian is not the roles you play in the home, but rather the relationships you enjoy with each other because of Christ. Why? Because a Christian family is a family that, by our definition, understands itself as composed of persons in relationship with each other and Jesus Christ.

We are worried today, all of us are, about the statistics I noted earlier. I could have cited a hundred more. We are worried about the erosion of family values and traditional family relationships. I submit, however, that the real enemy, the lethal enemy, may not be the identified enemy. The identified enemies of the family today are television and the media, government intrusion or the two career marriage, the acceptance of divorce as normative and the general moral decline of our society. These are identified enemies. What if these identified family enemies were not the primary, deadly enemy at all?

To use our beached whale image, what if the enemy was not the beach, but our inability to realize that a parasite has invaded our minds? What if the enemy was not shallow water, but the fact that something has crept into our understanding that is not healthy, causing us to beach our family life and die?

I want us to consider how we can major on relationships by looking at some very important principles for staying out of danger. We might call this a test on "How to Beach-Proof Your Home." I will state these principles in question form to help you think about your own family and its health.

*Question one:* Who or what is the center of my family? Is it a career? Is the center of your home a person? a child or your children? Is the center of your home a certain family member's addiction? Is it some school activity? The band? Cheerleading? The football team? You fill in the blank. Who or what is the center of your family?

The Scriptures continue to hold up before us the great challenge to place Christ at the center of our lives and the center of our families. To be straight to the point, if Jesus Christ is not the center of your life, the center of your marriage, and the center of your family, everything else will vie for center stage. Like a parasite, every little minor "thing" will wiggle its way into your being to such a degree you will find yourself spiritually beached. When Christ is not the center of every relationship, we lose our way. Ask yourself, ask your spouse, dare you ask your children: Who or what is the center of your family?

*Question two.* Is there healthy submission of family members to each other? I know Paul says here, "Wives, submit to your husbands." Do not stop there. Read also Ephesians 5:21, where Paul also wrote, "Submit to one another out of reverence for Christ." If you are majoring on roles — husbands and wives — and your goal is a wife's submission to her husband, I suggest you may be missing the bigger picture in the text. Is there mutual submission, in healthy ways, of your lives to each other? How are you saying, in your relationship to your husband or to your wife, "Less of me and more of others in the home, Less of what I want and more of what others need"?

That's the toughest thing in my life. My children could tell you that is the hardest thing for me to live in our family. Less of Tim, more of

Kathie, and our children. It may be challenging for you, too. Is there healthy submission of family members to each other in the home?

*Question three.* What is the love level in my home? "Husbands love your wives and do not be harsh with them." Does that mean that wives are not to love their husbands and children are not to love their parents? Of course not. What is the love level in you home? How is the "Hug" quotient? What about the "Affection" index?

In over twenty years of being an ordained minister, I have married hundreds of couples. Before I perform their marriage we have a couple of hours in which we get to know each other. One of the things I ask them is, "Tell me about your home life when you were a child." Sometimes, one or both of them do not have to say a word, I can read the answer right off their faces. How sad and empty it is to visit with a couple getting ready to start their own home who have been starved of affection all their lives.

A daddy may have been in the home, but daddy rarely if ever put his arms around his child, hugged him and kissed him and said, "I love you; you are important to me." Young women who sit in my study with their future husbands who have never had a daddy to hug and kiss them in appropriate ways and say, "I love you my daughter. I'm so proud of you." Many young women today are hurting beyond words, longing for daddy's love and affection. The same could be said about men and their mothers.

I suspect I may be writing to some older, adult children in whose lives there is a great pain because mom and dad for some reason could not put their arms around you, couldn't give you the hugs you needed. There is a big empty space in you. To compound the fracture, you can't go back and recreate what has been lost. But moms and dads who have children under your roof now can demonstrate love to your young. You can do something about that. Ask yourself: How's the love level in our home? Hug your kids, tell them you love them, tell them they matter to God not for what they do but for who they are. Don't worship them. For God's sake don't do that. But love them. How is the love level in your home?

*Question four.* Define obedience. The text says, "Children obey your parents in the Lord." Perhaps we need to learn a larger definition of obedience. Moms and dads, it's pretty hypocritical for us to say, "Now children you are to obey us, you are to do what we say." And then for us not to obey the authorities that are over us. That's why it's the height of hypocrisy for us to talk about the problem of alcohol usage among our young, while we have a bar in our home and openly drink in front of our children. Where is the obedience in the home? Define obedience.

*Question five.* Have I created a frustration-free environment for my children? I am fascinated by Colossians 3:21. Why? Because it is directed to me. When you find yourself in the Bible, you are wise to say, "I've got to deal with this issue. I've met myself in God's Word." "Fathers do not embitter your children, or they will become discouraged." J. B. Phillips renders the verse this way: "Fathers, don't over-correct your children, or they will grow up feeling inferior and frustrated."[6] Helen Montgomery translated the verse: "Fathers, do not harass your children, lest you make them spiritless."[7] Have you created a frustration-free environment in your home?

How many of us leave our homes each day to fight the world, the flesh, the devil, the government, the boss and everything and everyone else all day long? How many then come home to an environment that is frustrating and stressful, where you are not able to let your hair down and be yourself? Husbands and wives, moms and dads, boys and girls, people of God, our families are a place where, unlike any other place in the world, we have the right to expect an environment free of embittering, harassing, critical frustration. Think again about little Tyler and Melanie — up at dawn, daycare all day, home after dark — and how frustrating it must be for them to live more than two thirds of their week with strangers, only to have the leftovers from Mom and Dad.

At the risk of being redundant, let me say it one more time. Perhaps the identified enemy is really not the enemy at all. Whales don't find themselves dying on a beach because the beach said, "Come to the beach." A parasite finds its way into their brains and they lose their way. This year and every year, tens of thousands of American families will head for the beach and they will not know why. In ignorance, they will identify a lot of enemies, a lot of problems, a lot of reasons for their broken home. My best guess is, most of the identified reasons for a home's failure and death are not the main reason at all. Don't be one of those families.

Someone has said, "Home is the only place in the whole world where the people who live there have to take you in." For God's sake, for your sake, for your children's sake, find a way to make your home that safe and special place where relationships with God and others define the family. Put Christ in the center of your home. Keep working on this test. I'm working on it everyday. Work on it with me. Let's work on it in our homes. Let's create that place where God is honored, Christ is served and where we take each other in. If it is helpful, here are the five questions one more time:

*1. Who or what is the center of my family?*
*2. Is there healthy submission of family members to each other?*
*3. What's the love level in my home?*
*4. How do we define obedience?*
*5. Have I created a frustration-free environment for my children?*

## Prayer

God of Abraham and Sarah, Elizabeth and Zechariah, you love us so much that you bring us into this life in the arms of family. The nurturing love of others first shows us the kind of place to which we have come. None of us reach maturity without others who have placed their fingerprints upon us.

We confess that being family is far more challenging than the shallow plot of a 30 minute sitcom. In a word, we need your help. Too often we are drowning in the shallow waters of even more shallow family relationships. Rather than swimming in the deep and nourishing waters of family life, we gasp for air, crying for someone to rescue us from crises of our own making.

In your mercy, grant husbands and wives the courage both to give and receive your grace. Grant parents the wisdom to rear their children to know you, to love you, and to serve you. Teach us by the example of your Son that we are never more fully human than when we give generously to others the love you have given us. Through Jesus Christ, your child, we pray. Amen.

# Notes

[1] *National and International Religion Report*, August 22, 1994.

[2] See Judith S. Wallerstein, Julia M. Lewis, and Sandra Blakeslee, *The Unexpected Legacy of Divorce* (New York: Hyperion, 2000) for sobering case studies on the impact of divorce on children well into their adult years.

[3] Wade Horn, *The Houston Chronicle*, June 19, 1994.

[4] Kevin Leman, *What a Difference A Daddy Makes* (Nashville: Thomas Nelson Publishers, 2000), is a must read for any male rearing children.

[5] Roger Sonnenberg, "New Life for a 'Dead' Marriage," *Lutheran Witness* (December 1994): 8-11.

[6] J.B. Phillips, *The New Testament in Modern English* (New York: Macmillan Company, 1960), 423.

[7] Helen Barrett Montgomery, *The New Testament in Modern English* (Philadelphia: The Judson Press, 1924), 542.

# Beyond Wading Pool Friendships

Tychicus will tell you all the news about me; he is a beloved brother, a faithful minister, and a fellow servant in the Lord. I have sent him to you for this very purpose, so that you may know how we are and that he may encourage your hearts; he is coming with Onesimus, the faithful and beloved brother, who is one of you. They will tell you about everything here.

Aristarchus my fellow prisoner greets you, as does Mark the cousin of Barnabas, concerning whom you have received instructions — if he comes to you, welcome him. And Jesus, who is called Justus greets you. These are the only ones of the circumcision among my coworkers for the kingdom of God, and they have been a comfort to me. Epaphras, who is one of you, a servant of Christ Jesus, greets you. He is always wrestling in his prayers on your behalf, so that you may stand mature and fully assured in everything that God wills. For I testify for him that he has worked hard for you and for those in Laodicea and in Hierapolis. Luke, the beloved physician, and Demas greet you. Give my greetings to the brothers and sisters in Laodicea, and to Nympha and the church in her house. And when this letter has been read among you, have it read also in the church of the Laodiceans; and see that you read also the letter from Laodicea. And say to Archippus, "See that you complete the task that you have received in the Lord." (Col 4:7-17)

Of all the accolades paid Mickey Mantle at his death in 1995, the one I remember most is not the fact that he was, for everyone growing up during the 1950s and 60s, "Mr. Baseball." Though polio benched most of my baseball playing time as a child, I loved to stand at the plate and hit the ball. I couldn't get to first base without being thrown out unless the pitch was just right. In those rare but wonderful moments, I smacked it for what would be a triple for other players. For me, the big swing got me limping to first base and safe. How I loved swinging a baseball bat — feeling the power of connecting with a ball — the exhilaration of making a hit, reaching the bag.

In those idyllic days, the New York Yankees were the only team for me. Reared in Miami, Florida, where the Baltimore Orioles had spring training, I was a Yankee fan whose many New York born classmates bled pinstripes. Those were the days when PeeWee Reese and Dizzy Dean called "The Game of the Week" — "The Game" meaning the Yankees. Mickey Mantle was my baseball idol. I was smitten with Mickey Mantle for many reasons — his problems with his legs with which I identified being one. What I admired about him, however, was the fact that when Mickey would come to the plate, everybody knew he would be swinging. Mickey Mantle was "Mr. Baseball."

Of all Mickey Mantle's baseball records, including the fact that he holds World Series records probably no one will ever break, one memory, beaming from the events surrounding his death, shines above all others. I will remember always how the men who played with him spoke of their love for him. They were friends. They knew all of his flaws, they knew all of his inconsistencies, but they were friends whose baseball records meant far less to them than the fact a soulmate had died.

Think about it. Friendship is both a demanding and delightful reality, is it not? We all know how the demands of contemporary life strain even the best of friendships. And yet, for those who "hang in" there, friendship becomes one of life's enduring delights. Why is it, then, that so many struggle with developing deeply meaningful friendships? You may be one in whose life friendship has been more difficult and demanding than delightful. Frustrated and often blaming yourself, you have retreated from any prospect of developing another friendship that could, over time, disappoint and wound your soul.

What gives? What I call "wading pool friendships" are the kind of relationships most of us have with other people in the private corners of our world. They are few and often deeply intimate. Psychologists tell us we cannot manage more than a handful of deeply intimate friendships. For men, this is even more difficult. We males of the species, to use John Gray's apt description, tend to retreat to our caves where, alone and withdrawn, we sort out the ambiguities and struggles of our lives. Women, on the other hand, engage others in their quest for personal integration. Women "talk out" their internal conflicts, believing that such out flows from the soul enable them to find their true selves.[1]

For all of us, wading pool friendships are relationships where both men and women who long for community can connect with others without the demands of transparent intimacy. Moreover, these shallow water experiences allow us the comfort of knowing others are "there" without the obligation to go deeply into a relationship before genuine trust is built. All of us have and enjoy wading pool friendships. For some, the pool is a large, built-in affair; for others, it is of the small, inflatable variety. Wading pool friendships enable us to navigate through a crowd, knowing enough about others to make conversation, but not committing ourselves beyond our own comfort zone. In a word, we all need wading pool friendships. Even so, we need something from our relationships; something with others that is more deeply satisfying.

There is a danger lurking in the wading pool's shallow water. The danger is simple: we can spend all our time in the wading pool and never develop deeply meaningful, spiritual friendships with a smaller group of close friends. Just as we need wading pool friendships, we all — both men and women — need a person or two (maybe three?) with whom we can share our spiritual struggles, our relational disappointments and challenges, our very human fears and failures. The danger of wading pool friendships is the fact that for many today, the family–career–church–leisure squeeze is suggesting wading pool friendships may be our only outlet for expressing friendship. Some would say such shallow relationships are the best: no pain, no disclosure, no risk. This subtle temptation to place all friendships in life's shallow water, in my judgment, robs us of God's best and our best for others.

What is it about friendship that, when it is good, it is really, really good? There is nothing in all the world like a satisfying, mutually sharing friendship. Whether it is with your wife or your husband, someone at work or in your family, your neighbor or your walking companion, when a friendship is good, nothing else can top it. And yes, when a friendship dies, or when you simply cannot break through to another human being because of — who knows what? — it can be one of life's disappointing sorrows. When it's good, it is really good. And when it is bad, it is awful!

Friendship, perhaps more than any subject other than love, has inspired great poetry through the years. American poet Ralph Waldo Emerson wrote, "A friend may well be reckoned the masterpiece of Nature." And in another place, he wrote a line I thought came from my mother, but actually was penned by Emerson. Said he, "The only way to have a friend is to be one." The writer of Proverbs says, "A friend loves at all times." A book not included in the Protestant Bible, The Book of Ecclesiasticus, has this line, "A faithful friend is the medicine of life."[2]

We know it is true, don't we? When a friendship is good, life adds a skip, a smile, a wink that reminds you someone "out there" has you close to the heart. A strong friendship is better than any medicine known to humankind. But then, when a friendship turns bad, when it is difficult, it can become bitter sorrow. A struggling friendship can stalk you in the stillness of the night and even terrify you in the rush of the day. Do you see yourself? Believe me, I can. I have been there, fretting over a relationship that is not all it can be.

The Apostle Paul knew God's gift of meaningful friendship. His letters reveal the fact that he made friends wherever he traveled and preached. I have often wondered what kind of friend he was. In the last lines of his letter to the Colossians, he talks about some of his friends in beautiful ways.

As you read those lines, do you feel the strong bonds that tied Paul to his friends? To use our language, Paul had soul friends — brothers and sisters — who surrounded his life with their lives and around whose lives he surrounded his personality, his dreams, his failures, and yes, his faith. I have been thinking seriously about how to define this slippery but important word "friendship." What would be a simple definition? How about this? Friendship is a mutually enriching relationship that empowers both you and another to be your best selves.

Is that not what it means to have a friend — to be a friend? When you are with your friend, or maybe even thinking about him or her, the relationship is nourishing and life-giving. In the embrace of a living, dynamic friendship, two people feel so alive, so secure, dare I say it, so fully human because they have chosen to share life at deeper levels. Shallow water will not do for two people who have become authentic friends to each other. Once you have moved from the wading pool — where all of us are most of the time — into the enriching waters of deep friendship, you cannot be satisfied with only shallow water again. I wonder if this has been your experience?

## Dangerous Liaisons

Truth is, we all have experienced friendships that are not of the deeply satisfying variety. Some friendships, quite frankly, are draining. You know what I'm talking about. Some relationships with certain people leave us feeling as if the drain plug of our souls has been unscrewed and everything within us is drip, drip, dripping away. You know the drill. You find yourself having little pep talks with yourself about your next meeting with this uniquely draining individual who needs you for a friend far more than you need him or her. Your internal conversation goes something like this: Will she be in that mood today? or, Be careful not to talk about…. or, Can I handle another hour's conversation about his low golf handicap and all the money he is making? You know what I'm talking about. Draining, one-way kinds of relationships. Every time you have an appointment with this particular person, you have this "pre-game" conversation with yourself about how to cope with the next hour with an individual who believes there is a friendship between the two of you. Some friendships are draining.

Did you key in on Paul's language as he wrote about his friends? Paul referred to Tychicus and Onesimus as "beloved" and "faithful." Obviously, both of these men had the ability to encourage Paul and he knew it. They had made the difficult journey of finding him in prison and, in those circumstances, lifting the Apostle's spirits. If you have a relationship with another person that is chronically draining your spirit, I assure you that whatever you have, it is not friendship. Friendship is a mutually enriching relationship. Key in on the words "mutually" and "enriching."

To make matters worse, other kinds of relationships mistakenly called friendship are not draining so much as they are desperate.

Desperate relationships involve people who have unmet ego needs, who attach themselves to your soul like hungry leaches and will, if unnamed and ignored, take the spiritual stuffing out of you. These desperate people do not mean to do that nor are they consciously aware of what they are doing. They are simply starving for a relationship with somebody who cares and you, at this moment in their lives, are that caring person. Truth to tell, what they really need may be a therapist. They may need someone with whom they can talk about the unmet needs in their life other than you. And yet, there is a desperation quality to their relationships with others. And yet you — the friend *du jour* — do not have it in you to meet their needs.

There are many desperate people in the world today. Read the newspapers; listen to casual conversations around you. There are more cases of childhood scars surfacing in adulthood than ever before. With rising divorce rates, there are more abandoned, bleeding, desperate people looking for meaningful relationships. With the economic landscape as it is, there are more abandoned, forgotten, cast away people whose careers, once promising, are now no more. Parents are experiencing all kinds of desperate feelings with regard to their children. They do not know how to deal with the changes through which their children are going and the different behaviors their children are exhibiting. They are desperate, trying under the guise of friendship to work out their pain and helplessness. What do you do?

To be candid with you, few if any of us can be another's therapist. There are professional counselors who can help hurting people find resources for coping with the difficult experiences of life. And yes, let me hasten to say in complete candor, everyone of us has a desperate corner within the self. I do — you do — we all do. That said, there are some people who, longing for something to fill the empty places within, attach themselves to others as "friends" who deeply need a professional therapist. How can you help a person for whom you deeply care who is relating to you out of the this desperation model? What do you do?

I suggest you take a big risk — possibly rejection — by saying to your friend, "Have you considered talking to a professional about the challenges in your life? I cannot be that person. But I will pray for you that you might find that person to deal with those scars, to deal with that pain, to deal with the brokenness." Some friendships try to live in the drowning waters of desperation. Unfortunately, most do not survive.

Why? Because some relationships, thinking they are friendships, are down right dangerous. They are toxic and often deadly. Draining and desperate relationships can metastasize as a terminal cancer in your soul. You can have a relationship with someone who whines without stopping or is negative or constantly critical. To be around such dangerous people is like drowning in a perpetual gripe session about something. If you are not careful, that person will become toxic to your heart. And sadly, you may find yourself becoming critical, whining, even cynical. Conversations laced with sinister sarcasm and cutting language about other people are no place for friendship to mature.

You know, don't you, that there are some people who cannot feel good about themselves if they are not cutting somebody else down. Some relationships, believing themselves to be a friendship, can be deadly. If you happen to be in one of those toxic kinds of relationships, I encourage you to wake up and move on. The person whose dangerous attitudes you endure has many needs and needs many things. Most of all, a person spewing relational toxins needs professional and/or pastoral care.

## Two Marks of Healthy Friendship

Authentic friendship is neither draining, desperate, nor dangerous. Friendship, when it is good, is really good. You feel strong and alive; the other person is strengthened by who you are. That is friendship at its best. The good news is, healthy friendships are just that way. How do they come about? How are healthy friendships nourished and sustained?

Paul tells us in the text. It is not so much what he says directly, it is what he says around, under, and between the words he used. Paul tells us two simple but profound things about intimate friendships that can move us beyond the wading pool into the deeper waters of meaningful relationships with others.

**Healthy friendships are simple**

Throughout this text a relational simplicity bubbles up like cool water on a hot day. Paul talks about these friends in endearing terms. He calls both Tychicus and Onesimus "beloved brother," "faithful minister," "fellow servant," and "dear friend." There is a simplicity in his relationship with these men and women mentioned in the text. Though he never says it, Paul has a deep affection for the ten individuals mentioned here. Look at the deeply satisfying friendships in your life and I think you'll agree with Paul. When a friendship is good, meaning healthy, it has an elegant simplicity about it.

Healthy friendships are such that you take the other person for who she is and she takes you for who you are. There is no positioning, there is no manipulating, there is no gaming. What you see is what you get. This is who I am. It's pretty simple. If you find yourself in a relationship where you have got to be someone you are not, or you have to wear a mask that's not you, wake up. Healthy friendships have an elegant, relational simplicity to them.

Read the names from the text: Paul and Timothy, Tychicus and Onesimus, Aristarchus and Justus, Luke and Epaphras and Nympha (what a gift of hospitality she must have had. She put the whole church in her house. Let's try that on Sunday morning). These were folks with whom Paul had a simple but powerful relationship.

There are a handful of men in my life with whom I have a close, simple relationship. They know who they are. I will call them or they will call me, and we get together for coffee and a bagel, or a lunch with no agenda, or a conversation about an issue of significance in our families, our work, the church, or community. Our time together is not spent trying to posture ourselves with each other or figure each other out. Not at all. We laugh freely and, at times, cry. Our time is spent being with each other, listening to each other, and growing with each other. It is elegantly simple and deeply satisfying. Deep water friendships have this simple quality to them that allow the more complex issues in a relationship to surface in a non-threatening way.

Hear a fellow traveler say that if friendships are difficult and more pain than joy for you, "Lighten up." Real friendship has an elegant simplicity to it. Ask yourself this question. Where is Jesus Christ in this relationship? Why do I feel so needy and hungry, even empty inside that I have to dump on others? What am I refusing to face in my own heart that comes out as pain, criticism, cynicism, or anger when I'm with others? These are the kinds of questions all of us would be wise to ask on a regular basis.

The reason Paul, Epaphras, Tychicus, Onesimus, Luke, and Mark could be friends with each other was because they had found the Friend of friends. Jesus Christ had accepted them unconditionally. If I may paraphrase, Jesus addressed them and said, "I take you as my friends regardless of who you are or what you look like or the way you talk or the job you have or the clothes you wear." Because they were connected to Christ they were freed to be simply friends with each other. No game playing, no positioning, no pre-meeting pep talks, simply being. Healthy friendships, I think, are elegantly simple.

**Healthy, nourishing friendships are intensely sacrificial**

Healthy friendships are simple in that there is an "at ease" feeling about them, but they are also intensely sacrificial. This text — in such a profoundly simple way — percolates with all kinds of sacrificial images. These men and women worked with Paul and with each other in God's work. They had let go of so much in order to take hold of much more. Do not romanticize the first century believers. Far from being glorious and noble, theirs was a call to difficult living (traveling hundreds of miles from family and home to meet Paul's needs), spiritual struggle (agonizing in prayer and ministry for others), and even death. These men and women so believed in Jesus Christ and the ministry of their jailed friend Paul, they were willing to risk everything. The word is sacrifice.

Sacrifice seems to be drifting away from our common experience. I don't know if you have noticed it or not, but we do not talk much about sacrifice. I fear that in another ten years the only way we will use "sacrifice" is in reference to a fly ball at a baseball game. When you are in a friendship that is meaningful, when you are relating to someone at the deepest levels of your life, you realize you are giving yourself away. Some of who you are, if not all of who you are, is being poured into that other person with sacrificial but joyful extravagance.

Some time back, I went to the mailbox and found a small package from Amazon.com. It was so small, I thought to myself, "This can't be a book." Then I remembered I had not ordered anything from "the largest bookseller in the world." As I opened the small package, I found Twila Paris' CD "Faithful Friend" and a note from a man in the church I serve with whom I have a wonderful friendship. On the note, he simply thanked me for being there for him and then referred me to cut 4 — "Faithful Friend" — on the CD. In all honesty, I had not heard this song by Twila Paris before. As I cued up the CD and turned the volume up, I sat there listening to the song, reading the lyrics, and uncontrollably crying. The men that we both are — visible community leaders, professionals in our fields — he could neither say nor could I receive face to face the powerful message in that song. That my friend would so value our relationship to send this gift to me spoke powerfully of the simplicity and sacrificial nature of our friendship.

Emerson was right: "If you want to have a friend, be a friend." But if you want friendship to be meaningful and enriching and empowering, there is no substitute for the giving of yourself to another. Friendship is simple, but it's intensely sacrificial.

## The Next Step

Friendships that are elegantly simple and intensely sacrificial require constant vigilance. If a mutually enriching relationship is to blossom into a lasting, lifelong friendship, something must change in the way we relate to others. As convenient as wading pool friendships are — remember, we all need them — deep water friendships that define and shape our lives require something more, something different, something radical. Simply put, it seems to me we need to quit asking of relationships, "What's in it for me?" And start asking, "What of me is in it?" Such a question is almost profane to our contemporary ears. It's a near obscenity. "What, do something for others that I don't get anything out of myself?" The current law of the land says: Do for yourself first and always. This way of relating to others, defined in relationships at work and yes, even in church is, "What's in it for me?" Perhaps we should better ask, "What of me is in it?"

My dad told me when I was reaching adulthood, at eighteen or nineteen years of age, "Tim, if you get to the end of your life and you can count your friends on one hand, you have done pretty well." One such friend I hold in my hand and my heart is Dr. David Jones, Senior Minister of Snellville, Georgia's First United Methodist Church. David and I have been down several roads together as pastors serving in the same city, as husbands, as fathers, as friends. For over 25 years, I have been an ordained minister in Southern Baptist churches. Through these years, I have had the privilege and joy of serving with many pastors, ministers, educators, missionaries, and denominational leaders. In all of those years, across all kinds of theological and geographical boundaries, I have had few friendships like the one I enjoy with David.

Of course, he is not a Baptist. And no, he does not line up at every point with my theology, nor do I line up with his. Come to think of it, we have never had a serious conversation about infant baptism, church polity, the virgin birth, or the second coming of Christ. So what has defined our friendship? Quite simply, as best I can say, our friendship has grown in the fertile soil of presence. David is one of the only minister friends I've had through the years who intentionally pursues me as a friend. He calls for no apparent reason — just to talk, "How are you doing?" He has prayed for me and I for him in times of great stress and soul anguish. For eight years, we have shared the blessing of living in a city not of our birth, but of our heart. We have a friendship that is so very simple, but willingly sacrificial.

Another one of my close friends is Bill Curry, former head football coach at Georgia Tech, Alabama, and Kentucky, and now with ESPN. A few years ago, when Bill was still coaching at Kentucky, my mother clipped an article for me to read from *The Atlanta Journal-Constitution*. I remember the article well. Bill, being an Atlanta native, was having a tough time at Kentucky. In fact, this article was written a year and a half before he was dismissed as their coach. Simply put, the article was replaying the "Can Curry coach?" line Bill has heard all his life. You tell me. Given the coaches in Division I of the NCAA, who would you like your son to play for? I still would take Bill Curry — win or lose — over 95% of the field.

Bill Curry and I have rarely talked football. We just don't talk about football. Number one, I am athletically challenged and I would not understand anything he was talking about any way. Football is not on our list of conversational topics. Number two, we hardly talk about church. A lifelong churchman, Bill knows more about the church, its inconsistencies and failings, than most lay people. Even so, church is not a topic on our list. We do, however, talk about life and being. We will go two or three months and not speak on the phone or write when one of us will call the other for no apparent reason. When that happens, it is like we just left the last conversation we had. You know how that is, do you not? You pick up where you left off.

I have thought about that phenomenon often. And when I do, my mind flashes back to a conversation Bill and I had over ten years ago. We both were in Tuscaloosa, Alabama at the time. Bill was coaching football; I was serving the Calvary Baptist Church. In so many words, Bill reached out to me and I to him. Both of us said to each other, "I need a friend." And then he said to me, "If it works it will be good. If it doesn't work, we will both know."

Is that not how friendship really should be? Because you see, when you think about Paul and all that he did and the people he touched and the way the whole world is different because he lived, you have to say to yourself, "Who got a hold of him? How did he become the person he ended up being?" When you first meet Saul of Tarsus in the Book of Acts, he is selfish, egotistical, and almost religiously maniacal. He is climbing the ladder of Temple success. That's his thing. And everybody around him knew it. Paul was a climber, on the way up. But when you meet him at the end of his life he is pouring himself out for Christ and for others. How did such a radical transformation happen?

Jesus had everything to do with it. It was Jesus who said, "Greater love has no one that this. That a man or a woman lay down his life for his friends." Jesus gave his life in a simple but sacrificial way because he considered us friends. Is not that what God would have us do for others? And yes, to let others into our space to be that kind of friend for them.

Remember Mickey Mantle? I have a photograph in my mind from his funeral service at the Lover's Lane United Methodist Church. Do you see who's there? There are Yogi Berra, Whitey Ford, Moose Skowron, Bobby Richardson and Bob Costas taking Mickey's casket out of the church. I will probably not remember the .298 batting average, nor the 1500 plus runs batted in, nor the 536 home runs, nor the World Series records nobody will ever break. No. I will remember those friends who knew all of his flaws, but who cherished the way "the Mick" gave himself to them. What about you?

When six of your friends take your body out of some church somewhere, what will they remember about you?

Greater love has no one than this. That a man lay down his life, or a woman lay down her life, for friends. — Jesus

## Prayer

Eternal Friend, loving Father, your Son showed us the truth of his own words when he said: "No one has greater love than this, to lay down his life for one's friends." Forgive us, we pray, for being shallow in our practice of friendship. We confess to you that so much about us is self-centered and self-absorbed. Life is often brutal and unforgiving. In our pain, we fail to turn to you, our soul's best friend, and find strength to be the friend others need in us.

In the busy-ness of life, where we are shoved and pushed through crowded calendars like cattle through a chute, teach us to be whole people created in your image and saved by your life. Grant that we may be so present to those around us that we will be the friend to others you have been to us. Save us from shallow relationships that drain our energies rather than nourish our souls. May we find in you the good gift of nourishing friendship and then share the gift with those who journey with us. In the name of Jesus. Amen.

## Notes

[1] See John Gray, *Men are from Mars, Women are from Venus.* (New York: Harper Collins, 1992).

[2] The apocryphal Book of Ecclesiasticus, 6:16.

# Who Is Jesus?

He is the image of the invisible God, the firstborn of all creation;
For in him all things in heaven and on earth were created, things
visible and invisible, whether thrones or dominions or rulers
or powers – all things have been created through him and for him.
He himself is before all things, and in him all things hold together.
He is the head of the body, the church;
He is the beginning, the firstborn from the dead, so that he might
come to have first place in everything.
For in him all the fullness of God was pleased to dwell, and through
him God was pleased to reconcile to himself all things,
whether on earth or in heaven, by making peace through the
blood of his cross. (Col 1:15-20)

Jesus is the singular personality in history adored by many, scorned by few, misunderstood by most. Who is Jesus? is the question of questions facing anyone concerned about the prospects of drowning in shallow water. Scan both the near and far horizon of religious literature and you will discover that more books, more articles, more academic papers have been written on Jesus of Nazareth in the last 25 years than in the first 19 centuries of the Christian movement. At every point across the theological spectrum, from rigid fundamentalism to prosaic liberalism, Jesus is still the one with whom we all have to do.

Who is Jesus? Quite frankly, we are not sure. Yes, he is the first century teacher from Nazareth, the son of Mary, the carpenter–stone mason apprenticed to Joseph, the teller of parables, and the martyr of Calvary. But, dare we say more on which *all* could agree when speaking of Jesus? For example, the word "miracle" must first be defined and then debated. Did Jesus perform miracles which defy medical or scientific explanation? Did he, for example, walk on water, raise the dead, and feed 5,000 hungry mouths with two loaves of bread and five sun-dried fish? The room once unified is now divided.

Was Jesus born of the virgin Mary without the participation of a human father? The house divides again. Was Jesus raised from the dead on the first day of the week – the day we call Easter – by the power of God and into the full life of God? Was he, in fact, seen by Mary, Peter, Thomas, and, according to Paul's witness to the Corinthians "more than 500 of the brothers" (1 Cor 15:6)? The Christian house is now not only divided, but walls have been built and rooms secured for all kinds of meetings to discuss *that* question.

Who is Jesus? This is the question of questions not only dividing the Christian family today, but is also the question confusing both the interested and cynical public outside the Christian faith. In my judgment, there is no greater issue facing men and women of faith today than answering this seminal question. Why? Because who we believe Jesus to be "then" and "now" impacts our private and public worship, our sense of urgency in evangelism and mission, and our public "God talk" to a world gazing through the windows to observe what's happening inside the Christian house. There is no more dangerous water in which to drown today than in the changing tides of "Jesus" research and devotion.

Paul is no stranger to our question. Colossians 1:15-20 has been identified by scholars as a first century hymn of confession whose theme is Jesus Christ. These lines, no doubt sung by first century Christian believers, communicate that community's understanding of Jesus. Like us, they were facing the real danger of drowning in the shallow water of a thin and meaningless Christology (a theological term meaning "the study of the person and work of Christ"). If Paul thought it imperative to guide their thinking, what would he say to us? Let's find out.

# A Hymn Worth Singing

This early Christian hymn is unlike any text we sing today. As a musician, I have tried to put the words to music. You are correct in assuming music will go with the words, but the resulting creation does not "sing" like "Amazing Grace" or "How Great Thou Art." So, on what grounds do scholars insist this is a first century hymn? Good question. Three clues tumble out of the Greek text and tip us off to the hymnic quality of these verses.

The first clue is the use of the tiny relative pronoun normally translated "Who" that is not present in most contemporary translations. The New Revised Standard Version reproduced above substitutes the pronoun "He" for the relative pronoun "Who." For English readers, this is almost imperative. The use of the relative pronoun "who" is descriptive – signaling to the reader successive words defining, exalting, praising the subject of the text.

This confessional quality of Colossians 1:15-20 leads us to clue number two. This hymn is, both in style and substance, a confession of faith. Read aloud Colossians 1:15-20 and you get the impression that this text, much like The Apostles Creed, was no doubt quoted as a confession of faith by early believers. In these words, believers found both anchors for their faith in Christ and wings on which to soar spiritually with Christ. Two of many other New Testament hymn texts identified by the use of the relative pronoun and possessing this confessional quality, would include Philippians 2:6-11 and 1 Timothy 3:16. In each case, the words sing praise to Jesus Christ, whose life, death, resurrection, and presence in the lives of believers was the substance of living, personal faith.

The third clue in the text that tells scholars this is a hymn is the fact you can remove Colossians 1:15-20 from the chapter – read Colossians 1:14 and skip to Colossians 1:21 – and not actually miss the hymn thematically. Look at the text. Colossians 1:13-14 reads: "He has rescued us from the power of darkness and transferred us into the kingdom of his beloved Son, in whom we have redemption, the forgiveness of sins." Now skip to Colossians 1:21 and keep reading. "And you who were once estranged and hostile in mind, doing evil deeds, he has now reconciled in his fleshly body…." Do you hear-see the continuity in thought between Colossians 1:14 and 21? Having announced the forgiveness of sins in verse 14, Paul reminds the Colossians they "were once estranged and hostile" to God.

Why then does the hymn interrupt Paul's argument? To be honest, you would have to ask him. Paul does have a tendency in his writing to chase rabbits, only to return to his original idea.[1] When you translate Paul's writing from the Greek, you constantly have to make your mind stay with his original thought while you run with him through the woods of another idea. Here, Paul ended verse 13 by speaking of God's "beloved Son" whose gift to us is "redemption, the forgiveness of sins." Having written that, Paul then breaks out into a hymn the Colossians no doubt knew and sang often. He quickly shifts from being the writer of a letter to the singer of good news. Just as any preacher might suddenly quote a line or two from a familiar hymn to illustrate a point in a sermon, Paul quotes this beautiful hymn to anchor his understanding of forgiveness in the person and work of Christ. So let's look at the hymn in more detail.

**Get the Big Picture**

This magisterial hymn to Christ boldly asserts that Jesus Christ is not only God's Son, but in fact is the central personality in all creation. Eight times in six verses Paul uses the words "all" or "everything." The hymn dares place the exalted Lord as sovereign over all "creation," which is defined as "all things in heaven and earth." The word "all" rhythmically punches you over and over again, as the hymn drums into your mind and heart this one non-negotiable truth: Jesus Christ is first and only Lord of all that is.

Such a sweeping assertion is almost obscene to our post-modern ears. What? You mean there is *one* story that comprehensively holds all reality in its grip? A post-modern cultural pluralist would deduce, "That may be the view of that first century text, but such a view is only one among many worldviews claiming authority." The cry goes up from the post-modernist throng saying, "The Christian confession 'Jesus Christ is Lord' must be heard alongside the Muslim's confession 'There is no God but Allah and Mohammad is his prophet' and a host of other texts demanding equal time." The question lingers: Who is Jesus? Can we sing with this first century hymn of Christ's exclusive claim to be first, all sovereign Lord?

So much has happened in the last 200 years to unravel the Christian story into a million tiny fragments of sound, text, and meaning. Andrew Walker accurately and succinctly describes the loss of the Christian "grand narrative" to the Enlightenment story of progress and now to the post-modern script of competing stories.[2] Who is Jesus? was once answered in near-unison by those who followed him. Now, the question seems up for grabs, depending upon where you are as a reader, interpreter, scholar, follower, preacher, or skeptic.

This text does not back down from insisting there is a grand narrative, a big picture, in which Jesus Christ is not only Lord, but Creator, Sustainer, Redeemer, and Peacemaker. Again, Andrew Walker: "The gospel may not be located in the text, but it is focused there in Jesus of Nazareth, the person identified by St. John as 'the Word': the telling-forth, or self-revealing of God. This self-revelation of God comes from his very being, in the way that an only son uniquely participates in the nature of his father (John 3:16)."[3] By including this hymn in his letter to the Colossians, Paul wraps far more than his words around a familiar text. Rather, he embraces the whole story-truth-meaning of the text as the very soul of his own understanding of Jesus. Who is Jesus? Paul believed he was the central Being-Person-Lord of all history, all reality, all that was, is, or will ever be.

Such a sweeping confession of faith may sound foreign to our contemporary ears, but the hymn "then" is no less relevant "now." Let's go back to the first century for a moment. Then, the tiny Colossian church was speaking what they believed was good news to a religiously pluralistic world much like our own. From evidence both within and without the New Testament, the geographical area around Colossae was a greenhouse for growing new religions. There, the mystery religions of the East met the rational religions of the West. Turkey "then" was like America "now." Many religions offered salvation, mystical experience, healing, spiritual centeredness, miracles, and so forth.

Thus, it is not accidental, much less shallow, that Paul would include this familiar hymn in his letter to the struggling Colossian believers. To insist that Jesus Christ was the "firstborn of all creation," and "in him all things in heaven and earth were created," was to make the most audacious and, to outsiders, outrageous claim. Believers today will face no less scrutiny or scorn. People will be polite and even interested if you speak of Jesus in the shallowest of terms: great teacher, kind human being, sympathetic caregiver, friend of the friendless. Mark it down, people will warm to such ideas about Jesus in polite conversation.

However, when you add words like "Son of God," "risen Lord," "virgin born," and "worker of miracles," the conversation moves from polite nods to near hostile rhetoric. The shallow water of a distant, domesticated, and do-gooder Jesus gets a nod from nearly everyone around the punch bowl. When believers insist on the big picture, cosmic centrality of the risen Lord, the conversation turns suddenly silent, and yes, at times, hostile.

Who is Jesus? C.S.Lewis' now famous quote says it better than anyone, anywhere I know:

> [Jesus] would either be a lunatic on a level with the man who says he is a poached egg or else he would be the Devil of Hell. You must make your choice. Either this man was, and is, the Son of God: or else a madman or something worse.[4]

The first Christians staked their very lives on the sweeping truth contained in this six-verse hymn. Let's look at it in still closer detail.

**Source and Goal of Creation**

The hymn's major theme has to do with the fact that creation finds its source and goal in Christ. Not an isolated idea in the New Testament, the late first century Gospel of John would begin by confessing "In the beginning was the Word, and the Word was with God, and the Word was God. He was in the beginning with God. All things came into being through him, and without him not one thing came into being" (John 1:1-3). The anonymous writer of Hebrews likewise began with these words: "Long ago God spoke to our ancestors in many and various ways by the prophets, but in these last days he has spoken to us by a Son, whom he appointed heir of all things, through whom he also created the worlds" (Heb 1:1-2).

Why such grand, even arrogant language insisting that through Jesus Christ all reality came into being? Take your question back to the event of the resurrection. Clearly the New Testament bubbles up as both text and witness to the Christian community from the rushing spring of Jesus' resurrection from the dead. Paul was so bold as to declare that if Christ was not raised, there is no faith to believe, preach, or confess, much less a reality in which we live and into which we die (cf. 1 Cor 15:12-28). Someone has said that people will die for something they believe to be true, but is, in fact, false. People will not, however, die for something they know to be false. Because Christ was raised from death by the power of God, a new lens has been given the human family through which we view all reality. That lens is the polished diamond of Christ's risen life. Such radical good news changes the conclusions of more than a few textbooks in the library.

With great detail, the hymn triumphantly solves a mystery many first century people found incomprehensible. Simply put, the mystery that could not be explained was this: How do we keep the "unknown" — death, guilt, meaninglessness, ambiguity — from bringing us harm? Guess what? We struggle with it, too. The ancients answered that question with a pantheon of gods and goddesses; each one the source of a certain aspect of life. Thus, with so much unknowable out there, one's best posture was to placate as many of the deities as possible. Play it safe, cover your bases, keep the gods and goddesses happy.

The hymn demolishes this keep-the-gods-at-bay idea by insisting that reality is full of living things, but the creation of the one living God. Rather than needing to placate a chorus line of selfish and capricious personalities, the Christian faith declares all that is — visible and invisible — is the creation of One who dared answer the mystery by becoming, "in his fleshly body," the peacemaker between God and humanity. Creation is not broken, sinister, malevolent, mean, gone mad, or evil. Creation is God's work, now experienced in freedom, in which we can choose God and know grace.

Paul says as much later in the Colossian letter. The ancients — perhaps a view strongly held at Colossae — cowered in fear before "the mystery" of the universe. Paul used strong language with the Colossians in order to take all the teeth out of their pagan neighbor's beliefs. His desire for the Colossians was "that they may have all the riches of assured understanding and have the knowledge of God's mystery, that is, Christ himself, in whom are hidden all the treasures of wisdom and knowledge. I am saying this so that no one may deceive you with plausible arguments" (Col 2:2b-4).

Today, we face no less a challenge in living out our Christian faith. The shallow waters of contemporary life are filled with crystal nonsense, psychic "friends" who are really charlatans, religious stupidity disguised as healing, wealth, and power, and self-centered rituals leading people more into themselves and away from relationships with others. To say that Jesus Christ is the source and goal of all creation liberates believers to see all reality under his Lordship. "Christ in you" is "the hope of glory." Where is history going? What is the goal of our existence? The hymn holds nothing back. The goal of history, like its source, is Jesus Christ. The nihilists say history has no meaning. Christian faith declares reality's grand narrative has a home not in the abyss of nothingness or even the embrace of a comprehensive idea. Rather, the goal of history is a person in whose life we find our true personhood, dignity, and hope.

All who would dare live in faith, who long for deeper spiritual meaning in life, may turn in other directions, but only Christ extends nail-scarred hands and offers us not only a hope, but his very life. This great truth was brought home to me when I walked through a very difficult situation with a precious family in our church. Aspen Daniel was one of God's unique and precious gifts. She was born with Down's Syndrome and lived less than four years. In that small handful of time, through that one incredible life, I witnessed more of God, more of Christ, more of love than I have seen in my years of ministry. Aspen was a gift. I still miss her.

Now years later, I still have two pictures in my mind of Aspen and someone else. That someone else is her dad and my dear friend, Ken. The first picture is of Ken stretched out on a hospital pallet at Emory University Hospital in Atlanta where, only a short time before, he had given his own bone marrow so Aspen could be transplanted with the hope that her leukemia could be cured. There he was, my friend, Aspen's dad, giving his very life for the life of his child. He knew as we all did, the odds were stacked against the transplant working; the "match" simply wasn't there. But it was Ken's choice and daring love that led him and his wife, Aspen's mother Diann, to that decision. Aspen Daniel never knew a day in her life apart from the sacrificial, giving love of her dad and mom, Ken and Diann.

The second picture is also of a hospital room. This time, however, the situation was painfully different. Aspen had just died in the arms of her dad and mom. The transplant, though successful for a short time, did not take. All other efforts to reverse the aggressive leukemia had failed. Aspen had died. But there, in that hospital room, with her larger family looking on, Aspen was held in her daddy's lap as Diann reached around her husband to touch and love her daughter one more time.

Aspen was born into, lived embraced by, and died held in a great love. Ken and Diann were God's arms, hugs, and love to their precious daughter. There was never a time Aspen did not know generous, extravagant, and affectionate love. In a much greater way, with much more at stake, all creation is brought into being, exists, and moves forward in the embrace of Jesus Christ. Jesus the Christ is reality's source and goal.

**Up Close And Personal Lord**

Who is Jesus? The hymn having begun by placing Jesus Christ as the central being in all reality, now intensifies this claim by exalting him as head of the Church. Meaning? There is no abstract exaltation of Christ in the universe "out there." Rather, the exalted and reigning One cosmically is none other than the present and reconciling One relationally. God "out there" is a very safe idea for most of us to believe. God "here" and "with us" — Immanuel — is again where conversations with contemporary persons change from being pleasant to problematic.

Note three up close and personal realities now present because Christ is the risen and exalted Lord, "the firstborn from the dead:"

First, *the risen One is "head of the body, the church."* Contemporary individuals with spiritual longing often decry the crass institutional nature of the Church. Whether you are referring to the Catholic Church, the United Methodist Church, a Baptist Church, or even a "non-denominational" Community Church, the word "church" carries much negative baggage with many men or women on Main Street. Why? At the risk of greatly simplifying a complex situation, my experience tells me many react negatively to the Church for one of three reasons: (1) They were forced to attend church by parents whose spiritual commitment was at best shallow and inconsistent: there was little positive experience at home or church when it came to spiritual matters. (2) A negative experience as an adolescent polluted many positive childhood experiences; as a maturing person, the idealism of "church" was shattered and perhaps mortally wounded. Or, (3) They have had no "hands on" church experience as a person outside the Body of Christ, they see the institutional church as a organization that is largely irrelevant to their lives and the concerns around which their lives revolve.

Like it or not, our experience runs head-on into the text's confession. None of us — in or outside the church — can respond to the text apart from our experience with the church. An adolescent young man cannot find his life embraced by an institution that does not address his spiritual longings, confusions, hopes, and questions. A young adult woman will not place herself in an institutional setting that does not recognize her intellect, celebrate her hopes for leadership, or address her spiritual emptiness. Out of touch with the Church as the Body of Christ, many today are drowning in shallow water desperately trying to experience the Christian faith without the "hassles" associated with the institutional church.

The text offers us hope. The head of the Church is not an idea, a program, a Board or Vestry, or a human personality. The head of the Church is Jesus Christ. If you have turned off to the modern Church, I encourage you to re-engage with the Body of Christ on the basic level of your relationship to Christ. Yes, there are hypocrites and plenty of shallow, social-climbers in any number of churches across all denominational and non-denominational lines. Walk in the door knowing that and accepting that and be who you are "in Christ" to that fellowship of believers. They need you and you need them. Our number one loyalty is to Christ, who is head of the body, the church.

Second, *Jesus Christ is to have "first place in everything" within the Church.* Let me speak to active, participating church members for a moment. Being a "lifer" in the Church — Southern Baptist churches exclusively — I know how competing agendas can put the squeeze on a church's physical, financial, and theological resources. The church I serve is, to use my Dad's phrase, a "full service church." Our motto around First Baptist Church, Augusta is "if we don't offer it, you probably don't need it!" We do offer numbers of ministries, programs, and events where young and old, married and single, men and women can connect with God and others.

That said, the great temptation we face today is, in the words of Lutheran pastor John Stendahl, to communicate a "disincarnated Christ."[5] That is, we have placed Jesus in our windows, our hymns, our prayers, our Sunday School literature, and our covenants and creeds, but have left him out of our lives in relationship and service. Christ is "out there" somewhere, at a safe distance from our passions, our prejudices, and pride. This "safe" Jesus has little to do with the way we do life or engage others. He is safely tucked inside our Sunday rituals — thank you — and ignored the rest of the week.

Dallas Willard is Professor of Philosophy at the University of Southern California. In his book *The Divine Conspiracy*, he challenges us to see our lives as integrated wholes through which we express our love and commitment to Jesus Christ. In speaking of one's work, he writes:

> The specific work to be done — whether it is making ax handles or tacos, selling automobiles or teaching kindergarten, engaging in investment banking or holding political office, evangelizing or running Christian education programs, performing in the arts or teaching English as a second language — is of central interest to God. He wants it well done. It is work that should be done and it should be done *as Jesus himself would do it.* Nothing can substitute for that.[6]

"That" is precisely what the hymn in Colossians is summoning us to be and do. Because Christ is Lord of "everything" does not obviate the choice we must make in relationship to that reality. We will choose either to relate to him as Lord in the whole of our lives, or we will drown in the shallow, tepid waters of convenient religion we keep trying to convince ourselves is Christianity. Neither the hymn nor the risen Lord will let us off the hook easily.

Finally, *the hymn exalts in the work of reconciliation accomplished through Christ's death and resurrection.* Jesus' risen life is not offered to humankind as a special effects, "Wow!" entertainment for fickle spectators. For some, this is a disappointment. Then as now, some within the Christian family had bought into a mystical, highly personal "Jesus is alive and I'm home free" kind of thinking and living. The hymn hits such shallow and narcissistic thinking head on.

To the contrary, Jesus' resurrection from the dead was God's work to reconcile humankind back to God and to inaugurate the work of reconciliation within the human family. Is this not the obvious meaning of the hymn's line "God was pleased to reconcile to himself all things"? On the other side of the hymn, Paul applies this line to believers' work within the Church. "And you" (see him point his finger!), "who were once estranged and hostile in mind, doing evil deeds, he [meaning Christ] has now reconciled in his fleshly body through death, so as to present you holy and blameless and irreproachable before him" (Col 1:21-22). Let me paraphrase Paul's words. "Go ahead and sing the hymn with all you've got. Raise the rafters for all I care. But don't forget the work of Christ's resurrection is still going on as we practice reconciliation in the fellowship of the Church."

This the very same confession and responsibility Paul communicated to the Corinthians when he wrote: "All this is from God, who reconciled us to himself through Christ, and has given us the ministry of reconciliation; that is, in Christ God was reconciling the world to himself, not counting their trespasses against them, and entrusting the message of reconciliation to us" (2 Cor 5:18-19). In the Church, we celebrate a Christ-centered story in which the ending is still being told through the lives of all who sing it, tell it, live it, believe it. Jesus Christ, who is over "all things" including the Church is one in whose life we find life and in whose reconciling work we find peace with God and peace with each other.

Do not wonder why some churches and their members cannot seem to stop their bickering and lay down their grievances against each other. If you will look closely enough, you will discover that people professing faith in Christ have walked away from the One they claim to be following. Power struggles, political maneuvering, King or Queen of the church mountain games are all being played while Jesus is shut out from the fellowship claiming to be his. Do not wonder why so many Christian believers today are confused and turned off by the mere mention of the word "church." Both they and the churches they abhor have forgotten Christ, relegating him to the ash bin of church history. Such is the danger of a shallow water Christology that thinks highly of Jesus but does not follow him as Lord. There is another way.

## Christ in You

Paul boldly declares that the One who holds all reality together, who died and rose again, who is head of the Church is the very One who dares live in all who follow him. "Christ in you," according to Paul's understanding, has two dimensions. The first is hard to take. Paul believed that his sufferings for the faith in some way completed "what is lacking in Christ's afflictions for the sake of his body" (Col 1:24). Read the commentaries and you will discover that no one has even the foggiest idea what Paul meant when he penned this line. Scholars do, however, believe the verse reveals the sacrificial nature of Paul's life given to others for the sake of Christ. In a word, Paul saw the experience of prison, isolation, beating, stoning, you name it, as a giving of his life for the lives of others in the Church. Not that his sufferings would ever replace or compare to Christ's suffering on the cross for our sins — not at all. Rather, in laying down his life for others, he was bearing witness to the crucified and risen Lord.

In my judgment, so many of us are dangerously close to drowning in the shallow water of self-serving religion. We give our tithes and offerings to the Church that provides for our needs, our desires, programs for our children, comfortable buildings for our events, quality worship services for our "enjoyment." But ask people to give their money for sharing the Gospel with someone they do not know, may never meet, and with whom they cannot identify, and you'll discover how sacrifice is defined in the contemporary American church.

The cry is heard to be like Jesus, but so often, we cannot hear our own words because our wants are shouting down what feeble confessions of faith we make. Who is Jesus? Jesus is the One who laid down his life for us. Did he not say, "No one has greater love than this, to lay down one's life for one's friends" (John 15:13)? Flee the shallow waters of narcissistic religion and dare give of yourself and your resources to the Lord with no expectation of receiving anything in return.

As the Gospel declares the death and resurrection of Jesus, so the other side of "Christ in you" is "the hope of glory." The risen and exalted Christ is none other than the One who died and rose. In the giving of our lives for others, we experience a resurrection of ourselves, remade by the power of the risen Lord. The problem we face today is that we have a triumphalist Christology without the sacrificial "living out" of the selfless life of Christ. We want heaven without hell, glory without pain, blessing without sacrifice, and life without death.

The Gospel will not allow us to take the blessing without first experiencing the sacrifice. But for those who dare, for those who would give of themselves in sacrifice, there comes the blessing that is only known in Christ. Mother Teresa of blessed memory has much to teach us still. In her life, she found unimaginable blessing in her identification with the poor and dying, in whom she saw Jesus. You say, "I'm not Mother Teresa." No, you're not. There was only one. But you are the person God calls to follow Jesus — to be "Christian" — where you are. You have far greater capacities to give and sacrifice and love and bless than you realize.

Are you afraid? Who is not? The person of faith knows what it means to fear. Even so, the person of faith acts through fear in faith to bless and love in the name of Jesus. Who is Jesus? Jesus is the One around whose life, death, and resurrection all reality turns. Jesus is the suffering and crucified Christ whose cross is our hope for reconciliation, healing, and heaven. Jesus is the One who, if we would live following his sacrificial and loving way, the whole world would follow. Why? Because he proved he was the virgin born, miracle working, risen Son of God? No, not at all. Rather, if any person chooses to follow Jesus, it may be because they see in us, through the circumstances of our often painful and difficult lives, a willingness to give ourselves to others as did our Lord.

Who is Jesus? Why not answer that question by refusing to drown in the shallow water of a self-serving, romantic notion of a person who is whatever you need him to be. Such a Jesus exists in many people's minds. He never existed in history nor was he hoisted on a cross and raised from the dead. Who is Jesus? You tell me.

## Prayer

Our Father, you loved us so much that you sent your only Son to be our Savior. In his life, death, and resurrection, we have experienced your forgiving grace and now live in the promise that is eternal life. Teach us to follow Jesus who alone is the Bread of Life, even as we ask your forgiveness for the times we have eaten the spritual junk food of a Jesus made in our own images. Call us again to follow him who went to a cross of sacrifice where he gave his life to save us from our sins and ourselves.

Now stir within us a holy passion to be the presence of Jesus in a world drowning in its own self-indulgence. Cause us to be more focused on the lost, the hungry, the disenfranchised, the outcast, and less on ourselves. Make us a people whose lives demonstrate that Jesus is the Way, the Truth, and the Life. Amen.

# Notes

[1] One example among many would be Galatians 5:7-12 in which Paul conveys an explosion of angry feelings that interrupts his main theme of love and freedom in vv. 1-6 and 13-15.

[2] Andrew Walker, *Telling the Story: Gospel, Mission and Culture* (London: SPCK, 1996), 12-19.

[3] Walker, *Telling*, 16.

[4] C.S. Lewis, *Mere Christianity* (repr., HarperSanFrancisco, 2001), 52.

[5] John Stendahl in *The Christian Century*, Vol. 114, No. 36 (December 17, 1997):1187.

[6] As reproduced in *The Christian Century*, Vol. 115, No. 13 (April 22-29,1998): 432.

# Rough Water Theology

"Theology" turns off more people than almost any subject I know. Why? Because theology, as we all know, is the work of ministers, scholars, and other out-of-touch segments of the human family. Theology. I remember well the story about the rural preacher who proudly declared, "I never let theology get in the way of my preachin'!" So it is for many of us who play around in the shallow waters of this age. We fear some sinister, destructive, unknown theology floated by academic, ivory tower types whose sworn mission is to undermine our youth, destroy our faith, infiltrate our churches. When, in fact, what may be happening is that another's differing view of some aspect of theology threatens the safe, familiar, "homespun" philosophy bumping into the lonely corners of our mind. We are threatened and we are afraid.

Take a deep breath. Step back. Truth to tell, all of us — whether professionally trained theologian, lay person, or individual with no religious or spiritual commitment whatsoever — think about issues bumping into theology and wrestle with theological problems. Candidly, one cannot utter the word "God" and not color in the spaces theology requires. You may not be a politician, but when you think of the President, political thoughts color all the neurons around every syllable of thought in your mind. All of us — for good or ill — must come to terms with theology. We are all theologians. The challenge lies in how we think and act theologically. In my judgment, we deny or ignore the important work of theology to our own peril. In fact, we may end up drowning in the shallow waters of this age because we are out of touch with the theology informing our lives.

We are all theologians. Every day, we are shaping and being shaped by theology. Insightful German theologian Jürgen Moltmann, in an article titled "Godless Theology," said it well. "All who believe and think about what they believe are theologians."[1] Theology is public speech about God, faith, ambiguity, doubt, evil, hope, and so forth. In this postmodern age, more than a few are speaking as theologians: news commentators, politicians, educators, business leaders. To think or speak any God language makes us theologians. But are we drowning in shallow water, accepting uncritically the theology of others? Later in the article cited above, Moltmann reminds us that theology is not the exclusive work of Christian believers. Atheists, agnostics, and others "outside" the Christian family often speak theologically.

On the other hand, we who embrace and are embraced by Christian faith often uncritically accept the theology of others. Why, if it is on television or published in a best-selling book by a nationally known Christian writer, it has to be accurate, biblically correct, spiritually insightful, does it not? The third millennium is no time for Christians to be so gullible. Our faith in Christ, our witness to others, a needy world deserves better. As best I can figure, responsible believers are called in Christ to be intentional about the theology we embrace and accept responsibility for how our theology shapes the way we live.

Paul has been called the first theologian of the Christian church. What qualified him to wear such a weighty mantle? Where did he get his training? More important for our purposes, how did he develop and then communicate his theology? This last question is the one with which we have to deal in this chapter. If Paul was the Church's first theologian, how did he come to the theological positions he held and share those insights with others? Colossians 2:1-15 gives us some clues that show us this greatest of first century Christian intellects at work. For our part, let's consider this text a bit differently than we have others in Colossians. Rather than walking through these verses in a "verse by verse" commentary, let's roam around in them contextually and holistically listening to the text as we watch and hear Paul's mind at work not only in his words, but all around and through them. In my judgment, we often err when we only pick the words apart. As one African-American preacher reminded me, "It's not only what the words say, but it's the word between the words, around the words, giving shape to the words that make the text live." Together, let's listen in as Paul does the work of a theologian. We will consider Colossians 2:1-15 in three sections.

## Theology as Relational Work

> For I want you to know how much I am struggling for you, and for those in Laodecia, and for all who have not seen my face. I want their hearts to be encouraged and united in love, so that they may have all the riches of assured understanding and have the knowledge of God's mystery, that is, Christ himself, in whom are hidden all the treasures of wisdom and knowledge. I am saying this so that no one may deceive you with plausible arguments. For though I am absent in body, yet I am with you in spirit, and I rejoice to see your morale and the firmness of your faith in Christ. (Col 2:1-5)

Theology is work. Sad to say, the vast majority of believers today have a theology, but they hardly know what they have. Even sadder to think is the fact that this "lazy" theology — both shallow in depth and puny in substance — has so much of them. In another context, the late Henri Nouwen said, "One way to express the spiritual crisis of our time is to say that most of us have an address but cannot be found there."[2] We all have a theology. To borrow Nouwen's words, one way to express the theological crisis facing the larger Christian family may well be found in the fact that we all have a theology, but most of us do not have a clue what it is or what it means or how we "do life" out of the theology we have.

For generations, the majority of white Americans lived out a defective, relational theology with regard to African Americans. Throughout the 17th and 18th centuries, many Southern slave owners justified their lifestyle by quoting liberally from the Bible. Clearly, a preferred sociology was empowered by a very lethal and dehumanizing theology. The same can be said today in some quarters of the Christian family with regard to women. A narrow reading of selected Bible verses, culturally controlled by chauvinistic attitudes from both the first and 20th centuries, attempts to keep women in their "place" as defined by men. Like an earlier generation's acceptance of slavery, theology may be more informed by fear than faith. Those in power — in this case men — fear the loss of status, control, and role should women be encouraged to find their God-given calling and ministry in the Church.

A cursory reading of Paul's Letter to the Colossians clearly reveals the Apostle had an open, honest, and genuinely warm relationship with his readers. Paul did not write this letter to patch up a misunderstanding (as with the Corinthian correspondence), correct grievous error (as in Galatians), or justify his need to minister where and when Christ called him (as in Romans). Rather, Paul praises the Colossians for their "faith," "love," and "hope" (Col 1:3-6). Even though he had never visited them, he had it on good authority they were an active, evangelical, could I say "missionary" church. From all outward appearances, their collective, congregational theology seemed to be fully engaged with the demands and joys of knowing Christ as Lord. However — you knew that was coming, did you not? — there seemed to be a "feeling," an attitude, could I say a "spirit" in the Colossian church that would disengage theology from its relational roots to Christ, Paul, and other Christians. Freed from relational moorings, the Colossian believers were in danger of following any reasonably sounding idea that skipped past their minds.

Read these five verses again. Paul wrote "I am struggling for you" surely to communicate that though he was not physically present with them, he and others were present to them in the sharing of their Christian faith. Theology, hard work that it is, is infinitely harder when we attempt to "do" theology without being fully engaged with other Christians. This relational dimension to theology embraces many who confess with us "Jesus Christ is Lord." It includes first of all the visible Body of Christ where we worship and serve. Look again at Colossians 1:1-4. Notice Paul and Timothy are writing the Colossians — both of them put their "seal" on this document. Read again verses 3-4 and lock on to the pronouns "we" and "you" (which is plural in Greek). Read it out loud if you must to get the punch — Paul and Timothy (the "we") were in fellowship, communion, soul-partnership with the Colossian believers (the "you"). Theirs was a relationship bonded by their mutual love for and devotion to the Lord Jesus Christ.

This relational bond that held both writers and receivers of the Letter enabled them to speak and hear each other at multiple levels. Notice again in the verses above that Paul used the words "encouraged," "united," and "assured understanding" in referring not only to the Colossians but also the Laodecians who probably received this same letter (cf. Col 4:16). Later in the text, Paul further assured the Colossians by saying "I am with you in spirit." You do the arithmetic. Theology, like every component of the Christian life, cannot be done in isolation from the larger Christian community. As I write these lines, I am looking out the window of my guest room at Regent's Park College, Oxford, England. I am quite alone, except for the fact that all around my room — my life! — are men and women — many of them devoted Christian believers — with whom even now I am sharing Christian community. Just an hour and a half ago, I worshiped in Chapel with the Regent's Park community. Yes, I am writing alone, but I am undeniably, corporately bound to others here and wherever God's people are.

Theology is relational work. We Baptists pride ourselves on holding high the biblical doctrine of "the priesthood of the believer." This doctrine is foundational to all Baptist principles since Baptists first came on the scene of Church history in the 17th century. We believe that no one — no priest, no bishop, no Pope, no denominational leader, no pastor, no self-proclaimed spiritual "guru" — can deny or prohibit any person's access to or inspiration from God. Baptists have insisted "an open Bible" and "an open heart" is God's avenue for leading each individual in his or her spiritual journey. I agree!

Nevertheless, Baptists have never so embraced the priesthood of *the* believer to the rejection of the "priesthood of *all* believers." The text of 1Peter 2:9 begins by using the plural pronoun "you" when referring to all believers as "a chosen race, a royal priesthood, a holy nation, God's own people [not the singular "person"]." Even so, theology at its best requires hard individual work. Each of us must hammer out our own theology on the anvil of prayer, doubt, hope, even despair. Moreover, as theologians — remember, everyone is a theologian — we cannot and must not refuse to speak and live out of our own personal theological convictions. That said, none of us come to a personal theology without the conscious and unconscious involvement with others.

I learned to speak English on my own, did I not? Of course not. I learned English from my parents, my sister Jan, my brother Neal, and even my younger sister Beth, who later in life has taught me many wonderful words and framed them with an incredible personality. I learned

English on my own in that I am the one using my voice, my mind, my equipment to speak the language. Nevertheless, many people, from infancy to this day, have contributed to my ability to communicate using the English language.

So it is with theology. Paul will not let the Colossians or us forget that theology is personal, but it is intensely corporate. We have and will continue to learn from and be blessed by the theological insights of many. Some of those who can give us good gifts have entered eternal life. Believers would be wise to read one or more classic theological works like St. Augustine's *City of God* or his *Confessions*, John Bunyan's *Pilgrim's Progress*, St. Teresa of Avila's *The Interior Castle*, Brother Lawrence's *The Practice of the Presence of God*, and Mother Teresa's *The Simple Path*. For heavier reading — much heavier — you might want to tackle John Calvin's *Institutes of the Christian Religion*, John Wesley's *Journal*, Karl Barth's commentary on *Romans*, or even the much maligned liberal Paul Tillich's *Systematic Theology*. Theology is shaped by interfacing our mind with the minds of others who have engaged the Christian experience yesterday and today.[3] For Paul, absent from the Colossian believers physically, he nevertheless was bonded to them spiritually. Together, they were partners in ministry. Together, listening to each other and praying for each other, they forged their theology on the anvil of Christian experience. Together, they made their confession "Jesus Christ is Lord" by the way they lived their faith before a threatening and aggressive pagan culture. They lived, believed, served, and died together.

Our experience is no different. Contemporary partners in theology would include your Pastor, a gifted Sunday School Teacher, a person with whom you experience worship, a coworker at the office, your spouse, your child. You may discover that the college or university near you offers religion courses. Sign up and go to work. I often find my best sounding board for theological ideas are trusted friends who share ministry and life with me. My wife Kathie is one of the finest theologians I have ever known. She has a heart tuned to God and a sensitive ear to others. That combination alone feeds my heart and mind. Who else is available? I've learned much theology from my parents and Kathie's parents, our children, other pastors and professors of theology. Church members who have let me be pastor have taught me much about God and God's work and presence in life. Look around where you live and where you worship.

Theology is relational work and many are available to join you in your labor.

Two questions linger: How do we do theology? and, What are the fruits we can expect from our theological work? To those two questions we now turn.

## Theology as Confessional Witness

> As you therefore have received Christ Jesus as Lord, continue to live your lives in him, rooted and built up in him and established in faith, just as you were taught, abounding in thanksgiving. (Col 2:6-7)

Theology as relational work too often is the place where believers stop. The New Testament, however, sees the work of doing theology as the foundation for the living of the theology we embrace. One of the criticisms hurled at divinity schools and theological seminaries is that professional theologians are perched high in their "ivory towers" untouched by the real world of church, work, home, and the "daily" stuff of life. This criticism is not without warrant. Every seminary professor I have known is aware of this danger cowering in the halls of academe. Truth to tell, we who stand "outside" the academy are equally guilty of consuming our own theology.

This "navel gazing" tendency in all theology is sneaky, in that ideas can seem almost irresistible until it comes our turn to live out the implications of theology in our own lives. James, in his letter to the first century Jerusalem Church, warned his readers of the dangers associated with being a "hearer of the word," but not a "doer" (James 1:22-25). Our lingering problem as theologians is that we are shapers of words who believe naively that others, if they were as close to God, informed, intelligent, committed, must hold the same views we hold. Prominent in every church is the man or woman who makes a strong speech about ministry in the inner city, but has no intention of being involved in such ministry now or ever.

Henri Nouwen, quoting Bernard Lonergan, identifies this universal human sin as "scotosis:"

> Scotosis means long and fierce discussions about justice and equality while we hate our teacher or ignore the needs of our fellow students.

Scotosis means endless academic quarrels in a world filled with atrocities and much talk about hunger by people suffering from overweight. Scotosis allows church people to indulge in comfortable discussions about the Kingdom of God while they should know that God is with the poor, the sick, the hungry, and the dying.[4]

Theology is relational. Theology is powerfully confessional. Paul contends the work of theology as confession has no valid application apart from theology in relation to and with others.

In three power-packed verses, Paul reminds the Colossians that a sound personal theology is bonded to a strong confessional witness of Jesus Christ as Lord. Our mouth's confession of faith, however, is not what I believe Paul had in mind when he penned these lines. The New Revised Standard Version above translates the Greek word *peripateo* as "continue to live your lives." The word literally means "to walk around." In ancient Greece, the "peripatetic" philosophers were those who "walked around" teaching and living the philosophy they espoused. In fact, the word "philosophy" has become so removed from its original meaning that we now believe philosophy is something primarily thought. Not so. Greek philosophers where individuals who lived out the thinking they embraced. To prove the point, Judaism was viewed by the Greeks not as a religion, but as a philosophy. Why? Because Jews "lived out" their philosophy by refusing to eat pork, worshiping on Saturday, circumcising their male babies, and living with other Jews in neighborhoods of the city. To the Greeks, Judaism was a "philosophy."

Hence, Paul tells the Colossians they are to "walk around" *in* Christ. That is, they are do their theology "outside" their minds confessing their faith in the lifestyle, words, behavior, and relationships that made up their so-called "life." How do you do theology? You begin by living on the outside what you claim to believe on the inside. One question lingers: How is that done?

Paul tells us. "Rooted and built up in him and established in the faith." A few weeks ago — it was mid-spring at the time — I went into our backyard early on a Saturday morning to do one of the least enjoyable chores of home ownership: pulling up the oak seedlings from our pine straw covered natural areas. This last year was a bumper crop. The two more visible natural areas in our backyard were teaming with tiny oak seedlings pushing their way through the thick brown pine straw. It took me two hours — thank you Kathie for helping — but we pulled them all up. Interesting, is it not, how oak seedlings become oak trees. With every seedling I pulled from the moist ground, I noticed a two to three inch tap root already nosing it's way deep into the earth. Even in its infancy, an oak tree requires a deep-seated tap root to survive.

In the same way, theology must have a tap root firmly seated in the moist ground of theological inquiry. According to Paul, that tap root is a personal and dynamic relationship with Jesus Christ. To use our working metaphor, theology apart from active Christian witness is nothing more than shallow water splashing at the shore of God's mind and heart. Theology disconnected from a Christian lifestyle is mere speculation; intellectual musings about ideas that have no impact on the way the thinker or anyone else lives or dies. Paul's oft-used phrase "in him" or "in Christ" rightly orients our lives to the One who is "all in all." We who use God language and think God thoughts and endeavor to do God's work cannot do theology well apart from being "in Christ."

Paul then adds the words "just as you were taught, abounding with thanksgiving." There are at least two ways to interpret this last phrase of verse 7. The first is to key in on the words "just as you were taught." Many do. In fact, more than a few Christian believers today are frightened of any theology that does not agree with or come from the person or persons who taught them the faith. I recently met a person who proudly told me she owned an audio tape of "every sermon" sold by a well-known television preacher. Though I did not ask her, my hunch is she would interpret this phrase to mean that one's personal theology cannot vary from the theology one has received from another or, in a narrower sense, a theology that has been approved by one's mentor, teacher, or minister.

If you do not think this interpretation is alive and well, think again. Theology, as understood by many in both the conservative and liberal sides of the church house, often means "approved" theology. Those on the left ought be careful in harpooning the fundamentalists in the house for worshiping at the feet of their revered preachers. We who would never think of linking the "F" word — as in "fundamentalist" — with our theology, nonetheless have our own list of approved and quoted theologians. "Just as you were taught" all too easily means "what somebody taught you to think and nothing else."

There is another way to unpack this phrase. Read all the rest of the verse. "Just as you were taught, abounding in thanksgiving." In my judgment, Paul is not insisting the Colossians mimic or memorize his theology so much as he is encouraging the Colossians to shape their own theology out of their relationship to Christ and from the deep wells of gratitude. The word translated "thanksgiving" is the same word from which we get "Eucharist," the word many churches use to refer to the Lord's Supper. And what is "the Eucharist"? At the very least it is the remembering and retelling of the sacrifice of Jesus on the cross using bread and wine. The bread speaks of Christ's broken body; the wine of his shed blood. Is there a link here with the confessional witness of our theology?

How we "do" theology is powerfully glued to who we understand Christ to be and how we live out our relationship to him. Paul insists that the theological enterprise must be taken up by all who are "in Christ" who likewise have been taught to live out their lives "abounding in thanksgiving." Meaning? Abounding in sacrificial, self-giving ways witnessed in Jesus' life, death, and resurrection. Again, our confession "Jesus Christ is Lord" helps to protect us from the shallow waters of "what do you think?" theology. Theology at its best is bonded to Christ, relationally tied to other believers both living and dead, and expressed through a life that is following Jesus.

This confessional witness aspect of our theology is hard to miss in the lives of people where we worship and even those who, from a distance, we admire. Not long ago, I realized that urging my congregation to "get involved" in direct missions was ringing hollow off the walls of my own commitments. Had I served in the soup kitchen? No! Had I gotten involved, even in a short-term way, in our ministry to the homeless? No, I did not have time! Then, God's Spirit hit me over the head with my own preaching. "Tim, you are a hypocrite. You preach a good sermon, but you don't live a very convincing life." It was not easy, but I joined a group of soup kitchen regulars one Saturday morning and got involved myself in direct missions. I never worked so hard in my life, working over a hot stove, making soup with whatever donated food we could find, and serving a meal to hungry people. When I came home, I was tired, but it was the "good" kind of tired. I had the deep satisfaction of living out in very small way what it means to sacrifice (time, resources, pride) for others.

What about you? How do you do theology? Believers "do" theology in Christ, even as he has taught us through his sacrifice, his "thanksgiving" for us. One last question remains. To that we now turn.

## Theology as Intentional Worship

> See to it that no one takes you captive through philosophy and empty deceit, according to human tradition, according to the elemental spirits of the universe, and not according to Christ. For in him the whole fullness of deity dwells bodily, and you have come to fullness in him, who is the head of every ruler and authority. In him also you were circumcised with a spiritual circumcision, by putting off the body of the flesh in the circumcision of Christ; when you were buried with him in baptism, you were also raised with him through faith in the power of God, who raised him from the dead. And when you were dead in trespasses and the uncircumcision of your flesh, God made you alive together with him, when he forgave us all our trespasses, erasing the record that stood against us with its legal demands. He set this aside, nailing it to the cross. He disarmed the rulers and authorities and made a public example of them, triumphing over them in it. (Col 2:8-15)

Finally, what are the fruits we can expect from our theological work? This may be the most important question of all; it is also the most dangerous and risky. As we learned earlier, theology easily becomes a self-serving, self-justifying enterprise. History is replete with heinous examples — the Holocaust, the Inquisition, American segregation, apartheid — where the fruit of theology became poisonous, toxic, sinful, destructive. Having said that, however, we have no reason to pursue the work of theology if in fact such labor does not enrich our lives and extend the Kingdom of God. Theology for theology's sake is worse than shallow: it is hollow, vacuous, and ultimately worthless.

The lengthy text above is a difficult text to interpret even for seasoned New Testament scholars. My goal in the brevity of these lines is to capture the "feel" of the text as it addresses the work of theology. If you want to go deeper, I encourage you to use one or more of the many fine commentaries in print for a verse by verse analysis.

What are the fruits we can expect from our theological work? This text, while saying many things about the faith and including more than a few warnings to believers, finds ripe and delicious fruit from theology in the arms of intentional worship. The one, unifying purpose of the human family is to "glorify God and enjoy him forever." Such old language is summed up in the word "worship." All Christian theology, in my judgment, finds its purpose in leading believers into a deeper awareness of and devotion to Jesus Christ as Lord. Why do we involve ourselves in evangelism? So that others will join us in worshiping God through Jesus Christ. Why do we expend significant resources in mission work with the hungry, the sick, the homeless, the abandoned, the needy? So that they may participate with us, as one diverse and grateful people of God, in the worship of God praising Christ as Lord. All Christian work and witness finds its purpose in worship.

The text is complex in its structure and language. There is, however, a thematic simplicity to these weighty lines from Paul. Let's look at the text in three moves: a *warning*, an *invitation*, and a *celebration*.

**Warning**

The first sentence of the text issues a harsh warning to the Colossian believers to be careful so that "no one takes you captive through philosophy and empty deceit." Theology's goal is worship for the many reasons named above. Worship and theology are bound to each other for another very important reason. To use Andrew Walker's phrase, worship continually tells us "the grand narrative" of salvation given us by God through Jesus Christ. Paul's warning is strong: not every "philosophy" leads to life, many spiritualities are nothing more than "empty deceit," "human traditions" are a cheap substitute for Christ's death and resurrection, and glitzy rituals promising to link one with "the elemental spirits of the universe" are nothing less than entertainment. If you don't think that is so, remember Marshall Applewhite and the "Heaven's Gate" suicide cult of 1996. The Hale-Bopp Comet does not the Kingdom of God bring.

We are wise to remember that authentic, individual and community enriching worship breaks into our lives in the midst of many competing demands and activities. Believers whose participation in corporate worship is based upon the weather, a sporting event, or a child's fickle feelings are living out their theology. It is shallow, mind you, but it is theology. On the other hand, intentional worship bubbles up from our devotion to Christ as Lord and our living out of the sacrificial life of Christ. Worship includes adoration of God, confession of sin, the hearing of Scripture, prayer, the preaching of the Word, and often the breaking of bread and the passing of a cup. Regular worship raises an affirmation in our lives that sounds like a warning. When we participate in worship privately and corporately, we enter into the story of God's work on our behalf in Jesus Christ. Intentional worship bubbles up from a life that is keenly aware of other voices demanding loyalty, other confessions uttering words, other activities promising happiness, other people claiming truth.

## Invitation

Hear Paul's invitation to worship. Notice the next sentence begins with the three words "For in him." Paul, with perceptive brilliance, lifts high again the "in Christ" reality and then applies that saving "fact" to the Colossian believers' lives. Notice the words he uses: "you were circumcised with a spiritual circumcision," "you were buried with him in baptism," "you were raised with him through faith," "you were dead in trespasses," but "God made you alive together with him." Like a carpenter hammering nails into the frame of a new house, Paul's words pound the Colossians with the "you were's" until he comes to the liberating work of God who, by God's power, made them alive in Christ.

As we learned earlier, worship retells the Christian story through scripture, story, song, sermon, prayer, and communion. What is the heart of that story? Simply put, we were "dead," but in Christ, God has summoned us to life. Theology's ripe fruits are held in the golden bowl of these affirmations. Clearly, "the record stood against us." We deserve spiritual alienation, death, and hell. But God, "forgave us all our trespasses." Does anyone reading–hearing–believing this good news feel moved to worship? We cannot help but praise, adore, glorify God who has so generously and freely given us these good gifts.

The hard relational work of theology, hammering it out in our own minds and bouncing our thoughts off the minds of others in faith, leads to witness and worship where Christ is "all in all;" where we who are "in Christ" find our true home, a voice, and a story "acted out" in liturgy. Theology and worship mutually inform each other, feed on the same confession of faith in Christ, and find in their common life the praise which rightly belongs only to God. If you please, "orthodoxy" (lit., "right-praise") leads to "doxology" (lit., "praise-word"). Orthodoxy in its purest expression is not a list of approved doctrines people "back there" said were correct or accurate. Rather, orthodoxy is the living out of our theology of witness and worship.

One of my favorite hymns is "When Morning Gilds the Skies." The opening line of that hymn sings, "When morning gilds the skies, my heart awakening cries, may Jesus Christ be praised." Where theology goes either wrong or bad is when theology — liberal or conservative — loses its "in Christ" foundation. When rigid conservatives base their theology on the inspiration of Scripture and not the supremacy of Jesus Christ as Lord, both witness and worship are diluted, believers are deluded, and the Gospel is compromised. When free-thinking liberals build a theology on what is considered politically correct and not on the foundational confession "Jesus Christ is Lord," both witness and worship become rhetorical games and exercises in ritual. In both cases, theology becomes nothing more than shallow water musings, wading pool clichés. Paul's invitation is clear: Jesus Christ is worthy of our worship.

**Celebration**

Paul uses a well-known first century image to celebrate our freedom in Christ. The last two sentences of this section begin with the word, "He." Referring to "God" in the previous sentence, Paul uses a military metaphor summoning all believers to a celebration of God's victory in Jesus Christ for our salvation.

Several years ago, I spent three days in Rome leading a group from our church. I will never forget the moment our guide took us to a prominent point overlooking the ancient Roman forum. There, at that vantage point, you could take in the great expanse of real estate that once was the heart of the Roman Empire. What particularly caught my attention was a number of large pieces of sculpture dating from those years of Roman power. The guide said, "Look carefully at that piece over there and tell me what you see." I thought for a moment. The answer seemed obvious. Someone blurted out, "It looks to me like a large tree trunk covered with shields." Indeed, that is what it was.

But what did it mean? The guide proceeded to tell us that when a Roman general led his legions to victory over a foreign army, he would select a tree around which to nail the battle shields of the conquered foe. In fact, the English word "triumph" comes from the Latin root "*dre*" meaning "tree." This particular tree, covered with shields, is called, in

Latin, the "*triumphus.*" As soon as he said this, my mind raced to these lines from Paul's writing. Read them again: "He set this aside (referring to "the record that stood against us"), nailing it to the cross (the tree). He disarmed the rulers and authorities and made a public example of them, triumphing over them in it."

Use your imagination. Can you see the picture Paul is painting? In Jesus Christ, God has made a "*triumphus*" of the cross — a victory tree — by nailing to it our battle shields — our sin and opposition to God. The celebration can now begin. God has won the victory not by destroying us, but by disarming us of the weapons that were killing us. Salvation thus understood is nothing less than the liberating of our lives from the very destructive powers that are killing us. In Christ, worship celebrates this victory with every song, every prayer, every reminder of the freedom God has brought us "in Christ."

Theology. Everyone is a theologian and all of us live by the theology we have either accepted from others or hammered out ourselves with the good gifts others offer us in history, community, and literature. You may be wondering about the title of this chapter, "Rough Water Theology." Where is the rough water?

I saved that for last. Rough water theology is the most insidious kind of turmoil I know of. You see, rough water theology is only found in shallow water. That's right. You've heard of the phrase "a tempest in a teapot." You know it is true. A faith tempest of significant magnitude is experienced in so many lives who refuse to do the hard work of theology, only to find they are drowning in some shallow water teapot. Do not drown in that teapot. Develop your own theology. Build it upon the confession "Jesus Christ is Lord." And, as you work out your theology, bring it with you to worship. The deep water beckons. Listen and live.

## Prayer

God of all creation, with unimagined energy, you created all that is, forming galaxies from nothing and bringing into being humanity marked by your image. We live and move and have our being in the great ocean of your creative power. Thank you for making us with minds to think and imaginations to wonder; for wooing us in love to know you, to follow you, to worship you.

We confess that so much about our world is a mystery. We marvel at the vastness of outer space while being terrified by the smallness of our inner beings. More than anything, we need you to re-create us in the image of your Son, our Lord Jesus Christ. Quicken our minds to wrestle with every idea that impacts your creation and our common humanity. Deliver us from small answers to large questions, from thinking that we alone are the center of all reality.

As you created us to be free beings in your image, save us from drowning in the shallow water of simplistic, self-serving theology. Enlarge our vision even as you deepen our beings, through Christ our Lord we pray. Amen.

# Notes

[1] In *The Christian Century*, Vol. 117, No. 36, (December 20-27, 2000): 1328.

[2] Henri Nouwen, *Making All Things New*, as excerpted in *Seeds of Hope: A Henri Nouwen Reader* (ed. Robert Durback; London: Darton, Longman, and Todd, 1998), 60.

[3] A more comprehensive reading list is included at the conclusion of the book.

[4] Henri Nouwen, *Creative Ministry*, as excerpted in *Seeds of Hope: A Henri Nouwen Reader* (ed. Robert Durback; New York: Doubleday, 1997), 109-110.

# Life Preserver Prayer

In our prayers for you we always thank God, the Father of our Lord Jesus Christ, for we have heard of your faith in Christ Jesus and of the love that you have for all the saints, because of the hope laid up for you in heaven. (Col 1:3-4b)

Prayer is required nourishment for the spiritual life. Like worship, prayer bonds our very beings to the God who made us and in whose love we are being saved through Jesus Christ. What oxygen is to physical life, prayer is to our spiritual lives. Prayer is both intensely personal and inclusively corporate. One of my earliest prayer memories is standing in a circle with fellow four-year-old's as we joined hands to pray for missionaries whose names seemed as strange as the countries in which they served. What I remember most about that brief prayer meeting was a sentence spoken to us by our Sunbeam leader, Mrs. Dixie Purefoy. "Close your eyes and hold each other's hands. God hears every word from our hearts." Early on, I was learning that prayer is a "heart to heart" communication with God and often in the presence of others. Prayer is both speaking with and listening to God.[1]

Contemporary prayer seems to be enjoying both the best and worst of times. Scan the bookstore shelves and you'll find more prayer titles than in recent memory. My concern is not the number of prayer titles, but the theology–experience–perspective revealed within those titles. On one shelf, you can span the religious horizon from Thomas Merton's classic *Contemplative Prayer* to Benny Hinn's *The Anointing*. Both writers are talking about the same reality, are they not? The heart longs for relationship with God — to speak with and hear from the One in whom we live and move and have our being. Truth to tell, we will grab almost any life preserver thrown to us so long as it has the word "Prayer" stenciled on it.

Paul began his Letter to the Colossians in the context of prayer. Like most of the letters he wrote, he believed prayer to be the first word and often the last word the people of God need to hear. Before we revisit his lines to the Colossians, let's consider several popular attitudes towards prayer. I call these "life preserver prayers" because they normally tumble out of our lives when we are drowning in life's shallow waters, desperately in need of rescue. All of us at times are guilty of spluttering out "save me" lines to God. What we often lose in the process is the realization that God longs to have constant, spiritual communion with us. Going about our daily business without the awareness of God is sheer folly when we remember that God is present to us at all times. To quote my friend and prayer mentor Dr. Glenn Hinson, "God is always beaming holy love to us." More than a few of us have almost drowned in shallow water, desperately clinging to a life preserver prayer.

## Four Life Preserver Prayers

Just as life preservers come in various styles and sizes, so life preserver prayer comes into our lives in many forms.

### Noisy, desperate prayer

Jesus addressed this phenomenon on more than one occasion. In the Sermon on the Mount, Jesus identified two groups of humanity who pray in this way. The first group he called "the hypocrites" (Matt 6:5). Having been reared in the womb of Jewish orthodoxy, Jesus knew the prayer traditions of his people. It was the custom in that day for men to stand in the synagogues and apparently on the street corners and loudly voice their prayers to God. This ostentatious, public outburst of words was an attempt to communicate piety. According to Jesus, such prayers are nothing more than words heard by others. God is apparently listening for something else.

The other group Jesus identified as praying noisy, desperate prayers were "the Gentiles" who, according to Jesus, "think they will be heard because of their many words" (Matt 6:7). Not completely unlike the Jewish tradition in which Jesus was reared was the non-Jewish, Gentile tradition of praying long, intricate prayers piled high with "many words." The best biblical example of this phenomenon is the lengthy prayers offered the god Baal by the pagan priests on Mount Carmel. You will remember the story of how Elijah challenged the priests of Baal, letting them invoke their god for the gift of fire (1 Kings 18:20-40). The priests of Baal "cried aloud" and "raved on... but there was no voice, no answer, and no response" (1 Kings 18:28-29). According to Jesus, God is not impressed with our words. In fact, Jesus said God "knows what you need before you ask him" (Matt 6:8).

Noisy, desperate prayer is not an isolated, ancient phenomenon. People confess to me on a regular basis their spiritual desperation when faced with a difficult set of circumstances not of their choosing. Prayer, that God intends to nurture and sustain our spiritual lives, can so easily become nothing but a life preserver, thrown to people drowning in the shallow waters of life's changing situations. I know. I have been there and so have you. We may think that raising the volume of our prayers or increasing our prayer's fervor gets God's attention. Persons who have grown in prayer, however, have learned that God's attention is not something we need to get. Quite the contrary: we already have God's attention.

Noisy prayer bears witness to our belief that God is disinterested in listening to our prayers. We must raise our voice to get God's attention. By contrast, thoughtful prayer is mindful of God at all times and in all situations. Noisy, desperate prayer reveals an understanding of God and prayer that is weak, ineffective, and shallow.

## Self-saving prayer

This second form of life preserver prayer is equally impotent. Anyone who has ever experienced the rough waters of life — and that is all of us — know well how self-saving prayer works. Like the S.O.S. from a sinking ship, we cry out to God in times of distress, "Help!" Throughout my ministry I have walked into the Emergency Room and met people facing a greater emergency than the son or daughter, mother or father, receiving medical treatment in an adjacent trauma suite. In times of life-threatening peril, we instinctively pray egotistic, self-saving prayers. We seem genetically predisposed to do so. Like the stories of people who find themselves on an airplane that's crashed; our first instinct is to survive ourselves and then to aid others in the survival process. The human species has an incredible, God-given will to survive all manner of life-threatening situations.

That said, saving ourselves seems so far from God's primary purpose in prayer. Jonah learned that in the belly of a fish. Fleeing from God's higher purposes for him, Jonah bought passage on a ship not bound for his God-given destiny, but rather for the farthest point known to ancient people: the edge-of-the-world city of Tarshish. A violent storm churned the Mediterranean Sea, his shipmates identified Jonah as the cause and summarily threw him overboard. God provided a great fish to swallow the fugitive prophet and there, in the smelly gut of a fish, Jonah prayed a prayer that is the prototype of all self-saving prayers. Hear selected lines from that ancient distress signal (Jonah 2:2, 5, 7):

I called to the Lord out of my distress,
    and he answered me;
out of the belly of Sheol I cried,
    and you heard my voice....
The waters closed in over me;
    the deep surrounded me;...
As my life was ebbing away,
    I remembered the Lord.

Read the entire prayer in Jonah 2:2-9 and notice how many times the words "me," "I," and "my" appear in the first five verses of the prayer. Not until Jonah prays "I remembered the Lord" does the prayer shift from "Save me!" to thanksgiving and praise. In a word, self-saving prayers are narcissistic; they turn all the spotlights in the room on ourselves.

Right now, I think I know what's going through your mind. "Are you saying we should not pray to God when we find ourselves in life-threatening situations?" No, I did not say that. What I am saying is if dire situations are the *only* or *primary* times in which you pray, you have not only missed the meaning of prayer, but you have cheapened the relationship God longs to have with you. Self-saving prayers are shallow waters in which to experience the fuller life of God.

## "Treading water" prayer

Those of us who have had swimming lessons at some time in our lives know that one of the skills we learn is the ability to tread water. Swimming instructors are quick to tell you that in times of distress or physical exhaustion, the best thing you can do is not panic; simply tread water until you regain some of your strength. When you are in deep water, far from shore, companions, or help, treading water can save your life.

What happens, though, when we experience prayer as "treading water" is that we may forget that our goal is not to stay where we are but to move toward the safety of shore or a rescue boat we hope comes our way. Treading water is not the same thing as swimming in the sea. And yet, many believers never grow beyond treading water, just getting by, "now I lay me down to sleep" prayers they learned as children. This "treading water" phenomenon appears in all kinds of ways in our prayer lives. Let me illustrate from my own experience.

Stock beginnings and endings to our prayers so often reveal the treading water phenomenon. The Bible reveals that the Trinitarian God enjoys a plethora of names given God by humankind. "Father," "God of heaven and earth," "Almighty," "Loving Savior," "Redeemer," "Lord," "Friend of Sinners," "Alpha and Omega," "Lamb of God," "Lord Jesus Christ," and "Spirit of God," are only a few of the many titles we can use to address God in prayer. The same can be said of the way we close our prayers. As a child, I was taught always to pray "in Jesus' Name." As an adult, I've learned that my entire relationship to God is not possible apart from being "in Christ." Thus, when believers pray, we pray "in Christ" because that is the relationship we enjoy with God.

Like prayer's beginning, we can close our prayers with any one of a host of beautiful word "ribbons" adorning our conversation with God. "In Jesus' Name," "in the Name of the One who loved us and gave himself for us," "in the Name of Jesus, the Christ," and "in the Name of your Son and our Savior" are but a few of many ways we can conclude our times of prayer. Use your imagination in prayer; develop your own unique, beautiful ways of speaking with God. Refuse to tread water.

Another convenient trap many evangelical Christians fall into is the use of "tag" phrases here and there in our prayers. Some well-known examples would include "and forgive us of all our sins," "bless the missionaries" — all of them!, "heal the sick," "help the poor," "feed the hungry," and "bless the church." One line, rote wonders punctuate too many of our prayers. Don't misunderstand me. We must pray for the missionaries and surely we know the confession of sin is integral to our relationship with God. My concern, however, is with the use of trite, packaged phrases that sound good to our ears but have no substance to them. What specific sins need confessing to God? Pray for one or two missionaries by name and ask God to meet specific needs you know they have. If you choose to pray for the hungry, don't forget to ask God to focus your resources and time in actual ministry to the hungry. Treading water prayers can be very shallow; appeasing our own conscience but doing little to move us into the deeper waters of ministry.

I think you get the idea. Keeping our feet moving underwater is a way to survive at sea. Treading water prayers, however, are no way to maintain much less mature a relationship with God. Dare to deepen your vocabulary, enlarge your horizons, and pray specifically that God will not only meet needs, but use you in being God's presence and love to others whose needs you bring to God.

**Prayer that "drifts with the tide"**

We pray, and often, but chiefly in response to something external to our lives. The worn-out response "I'll be praying for you" often becomes the way we respond to the situations presented to us by others. A friend has lost her job — "I'll be praying for you." Or, a friend's brother has been diagnosed with leukemia — "I'll be praying for him." Or, the family down the street has been in a serious automobile accident — "I'll be praying for you." The situation at the moment sets up "drift with the tide" prayer rather than the life of prayer bringing to God petitions for hope, healing, or serenity in the lives of those we know and love. External situations push the "Prayer" button and we promptly respond.

This way of relating to God may best be illustrated by the "Dial a Prayer" phenomenon still prevalent in many parts of the United States. Normally based in smaller communities, clergy or lay people record a prayer for the day you can hear by dialing a telephone number. Without question, this ministry gives strength to many who find the daily prayers helpful in their spiritual journey. My concern is the way we bring the "Dial a Prayer" mentality into our personal communion with God. Various prayers are carefully recorded in our minds which, depending on where the tide is taking us today, we "dial up" and send off to God. The shifting tides of life determine when and how we pray.

You tell me. Is this or any of the other life-preserver prayers, God's design for our spiritual lives? Granted, dozens of personalities we meet in the Bible rattled off similar desperate messages to God in times of crisis. One thinks of King Hezekiah's prayer for healing (2 Kings 20:1-7), the Children of Israel's complaints against God and Moses (Ex 14:10-14), or the psalmists who cried out for God's deliverance (Ps 22:1-2; 35:17; 102; 1-11). Prayers asking God's swift rescue in times of peril are not only appropriate, but often the only prayer on our lips. The shallow side of all this, however, finds its way into our lives as the *primary* way in which we pray. Life-preserver prayers may be the required prayer for the moment. Nevertheless, we will drown in shallow water if they sound the dominant chord of our prayer life. There must be a better way of living in relationship with God that keeps us from such shallow water drownings.

## God Gives Better Gifts

Paul's simple testimony of prayer given the Colossian Christians offers us a profound insight into the life and experience of prayer. Using words dear to Paul's heart, he speaks of the lasting gifts of faith, love, and hope dynamically present in the Colossian church. Note the beautiful prayer relationship with God and the Colossian believers Paul expressed in Colossians 1:3-4b.

Faith, love, hope. You will remember that Paul concluded the beautiful poem to God's love in 1 Corinthians 13 with similar language. "And now faith, hope, and love abide, these three; and the greatest of these is love" (1 Cor 13:13). In this text, though love is the second of three virtues Paul praises within the Colossian church, it is first in terms of textual importance. Often, the ancients would place the primary idea in the middle of two other significant ideas. Here, faith and hope hold the supreme gift of love (the Greek word *agape*) in their embrace.

Meaningful, deep-water prayer bubbles up from the springs of faith, hope, and love in our lives. In fact, prayer as communion with God is difficult if not impossible without the experience of relationship with God in whom we come to know the meaning of these precious gifts. In this text, Paul reminds the Colossians that his and Timothy's prayers for them were possible and even empowered by their knowledge of the common life in Jesus Christ they shared. Note carefully that Paul expressed no desperate, frantic, or selfish attitude in offering this testimony to his prayers for the Colossians. Rather, he saw prayer as the bond that united him to this community of believers. Prayer bonded them to God and to each other in their common life of faith, hope, and love in Jesus Christ. Let's take a closer look at these three gifts in the fuller life of prayer.

**Faith**

The Greek word for faith is *pistis*. What you may not know is that this noun is built on the verb *pisteuo* which means "to believe." Too often, we strap faith to it's "noun" foundation and thus shackle it to a rock that cannot live and move and impact our lives. For Christians, faith is not something you have; faith is something you *are* — the spiritual soil out of which you act in the Name of Christ. When Paul told the Colossians of his gratitude for their "faith," he was not speaking of some static, sterile doctrine to which they had given mental assent. To the contrary, Paul was referring to a living, vital, life-giving, grace-sharing experience "in Christ." Faith is the wind kissing your face, not the word "wind" in a book; faith is cool water quenching your thirst, not "water" in a dictionary; faith is the tender hug of a loving spouse, not h-u-g in a crossword puzzle. Faith is the dynamic, living reality in which we know God and experience God's presence in our lives.

So it is with prayer. Prayer rooted in faith is always a living, dynamic reality in our lives. This is the only meaning Paul could have possibly had when he admonished the Thessalonians to "pray without ceasing" (1 Thess 5:17). Refuse to imagine a monastic church, holed up in private cells, only thinking of God while living on bread and water. No! Paul knew the life of prayer was an ongoing relationship with God that begins with the simple words "I believe" (*pisteuo*). Put the picture in your own experience. When you say to your son or daughter, "I believe in you!" What are you communicating? Some static, lifeless, antiseptic cliché to make you feel better? Of course not! Rather, to say "I believe in you!" to someone you love is to invest deeply in that life all the affirmation, support, and encouragement you can give. To use another word we find often in the New Testament, it is to "grace" that life with energy, courage, and passion.

The deeper life of prayer calls us to become verbal believers. Not that we use more words — you will remember that Jesus told us words are not the key — but that we would dare transform the noun "faith" into a verb — becoming verbal — in living out the words that comprise our Christian confession. Eliza Doolittle, of "My Fair Lady" fame, tries in vain to get the crusty-souled Henry Higgins to get over his obsession with her words to see her; the person behind the cockney slang wanting a tender touch, an understanding heart, a compassionate look. Words carefully gathered from a dusty dictionary or brought from the tattered clichés of memorized prayers will not connect us with the living God. Prayer lives in the deep waters of verbal faith.

**Love**

*Agape* is the Greek word for love. Preferred by Paul to all other words to describe the passionate, pursuing reality we meet in Jesus Christ, Paul told the Corinthians love is not only the greatest gift, it is the supreme gift worth desiring from God (1 Cor 12:31; 14:1). Love is, in my judgment, the most slippery, abused, and polluted word in contemporary English. In the same breath, we express our love for chocolate cake, our children, and God. Surely there is a distinction.

In Paul's expression of gratitude for the Colossians, he told them that in his prayers, he constantly thanked God for the love this small band of believers had "for all the saints." How is that possible? How could a tiny community of Christian believers in the inland city of Colossae have such a love? Let me ask the question another way: What of God's love do we meet in the life of prayer that connects us to "all saints" everywhere? This one line holds rich resources for deepening our prayer lives while insulating us from shallow water drowning.

"All the saints" has two meanings in this text. The first takes us back to Colossians 1:2 where Paul addressed the letter "To the saints and faithful brothers and sisters in Christ in Colossae." In this verse, "the saints" are not dead believers who have entered the larger experience of life eternal. Rather, "the saints" surely referred to the fact the Colossian believers genuinely loved each other. Their fellowship was short on rancor and discord and long on affection and affirmation. A second meaning of "saints" refers to the larger Christian family beyond the boundaries of the Colossian church. Though small, the Colossian believers had learned early on that God's family is much larger than their own community of believers. In fact, the Colossians had learned something contemporary believers too often forget. God's family is geographically dispersed and theologically diverse. Happy is the individual and church that can celebrate God's people wherever or whoever they are. "The saints" to whom Paul referred included all those who have said "Jesus Christ is Lord."

Some are wondering about the Roman Catholic concept of "saints" as those who have gone before us into eternity and canonized by the Church as "saints." The Bible draws a much more inclusive picture. In fact, the New Testament indicates that all believers who have preceded us in death are saints "with the Lord" in the fuller Kingdom of God even as they were on earth. The word, in its base meaning, is literally translated "holy ones" or "set apart ones." Saints are not people walking around with their hands folded under a glowing halo. Rather, saints are persons who have been made new in Jesus Christ by the power and work of God's Spirit. Saints are ordinary human beings whose lives are being transformed by the grace of God. Saints are sinners whose sin status has been named and in whose lives sin is becoming less and less while Christ is becoming more and more. Saints, put simply, are children of God by grace through faith in Jesus Christ (Eph 2:8-10).

Now that we've gotten a handle on the word "saints," let's apply Paul's use of the word *agape*-love to our experience of prayer. Notice that Paul praised the Colossians because their love was able to embrace "all the saints." Deep water prayer, at the very least, has no time for provincial or narrow-minded checklists of "insiders" and "outsiders" (We will pick up this topic in Chapter 10). For now, however, at the very beginning of this letter, Paul clearly applauds the Colossian's largesse of including all who know Christ as "brothers and sisters" in love.

In recent years, as I have lived through a very painful and intense schism in the Southern Baptist Convention, I have become more burdened for the fact that persons on both sides of the denominational conflict have used words, slogans, epithets, clichés, and theological "checklists" to divide Baptists from each other. I have been as guilty as others in labeling individuals "fundamentalist," "conservative," or "moderate." In doing so, I have used words to control my relationship or lack of relationship with other believers. In complete candor, we cannot be individually anything other than what our conscience allows us to be under the lordship of Christ. Wherever that places one on the theological spectrum ought have nothing to do with where that places one in relationship to others. Across our country, other denominations have and are experiencing similar conflict. I continue to ask: When will we put down our words and take up our arms to embrace each other in love, acknowledging our diversity while affirming our devotion to Jesus as Lord?

The Southern Baptist denominational "battle" has many casualties. Pastoral, missionary, and educational careers have been crippled or destroyed all under the banner of a shallow, unloving, and impersonal slogan called "theological purity." In God's name, the entire Body of Christ in every denomination must come to the place where we pray for each other as brothers and sisters, asking God to purify our hearts more than our theology, our attitudes more than our doctrinal positions, and our mouths more than our denominational loyalty. I have made a pledge to myself and in the presence of others I encourage you to make with me. Do not speak unkindly of another Christian believer who is living out the confession "Jesus Christ is Lord." If you disagree with what another believer has said or done, speak to them your concerns, not about them to others. Pray for those with whom you disagree, not that God will change their minds about an issue, but rather that God will change your heart's attitude toward your brother or sister.

Deep water prayer is comprehensive and inclusive in its embracing of all God's purposes and people. All who are "saints," who have submitted their lives to the Lordship of Christ, are partners with us in shining the light of the Gospel in this world of increasing darkness. I am convinced God needs every delivery system human minds can conceive, human hands can use, and human relationships can implement to communicate Good News to planet earth. Isn't it time we stop using words to crush each other and instead, join God in confronting our broken world with the Gospel of Jesus Christ? Only love can lead us to answer that question in the affirmative. And only the gift of hope can give us such a longing.

## Hope

The final word Paul used in praising the Colossians' commitment to Jesus Christ was hope. The verse numbered Colossians 1:5 begins in the New Revised Standard Version with the word "because." The late Cambridge New Testament scholar C. F. D. Moule reminds us that in these verses, "faith" and "love" find their life in the hope — the expectation — of God's final triumph in Jesus Christ. Linking these words together, dependent as they are on hope, communicates "the Christian confidence that, in Christ, God's way of love 'has the last word'."[2]

What would happen in our personal and corporate life of prayer if we believed God will always have the last word? Like faith, hope is not some static, lifeless abstraction Christian believers "ought" to have. Paul's face would turn red in anger if he believed such an idea was his legacy to us in the 21st century. And yet we live and speak and pray, drowning in shallow water, as if hope is exactly that — nice, but powerless; expected, but underwhelming; important, but not urgent. "I hope so" stuck on a sentence is about as glib and gutless a remark as "wishing upon a star" is in response to Jiminy Cricket's crooning. Christian hope is faith and love's life source even as a bubbling spring feeds a crystal clear pond teaming with fish. Paul knew hope to be the spiritual energy empowering his life in Christ. Thus he could write to the Colossians, "Christ in you, the hope of glory" (Col 1:27).

Life sustaining prayer bubbles up from the deep springs of hope in the living realities — the verbal expressions — of faith and love. If you are drowning in the shallow waters of life-preserver prayer, God offers you a great and lasting gift in the larger realities of faith, love, and hope. Prayer, held by such God-given gifts, becomes the transforming and energizing reality in which we find our spiritual lives nurtured and sustained. Like the oxygen we need to sustain our physical lives, prayer fed by faith, love, and hope empowers our spiritual lives to live in Christ, for Christ, and with Christ.

You may rightly ask: How do you know this to be true? I know it to be true because the man who wrote the Colossians about faith, love, and hope did so under the most difficult and dire of circumstances. If anyone in human history had a right to fire off desperate life-preserver prayers for personal deliverance it was the apostle Paul. So confident was Paul in the power of prayer, he said nothing about his imprisonment save one throw away line at the end of the Colossian letter: "Remember my chains" (Col 4:18). Paul's prayer focus was on Jesus Christ and others. He found great strength in encouraging the Colossians in their ministry for Christ, praising them for their faithfulness, and guiding them in their quest for spiritual maturity. Rather than expending his prayers on himself, whining and complaining about his circumstances, or communicating God was nothing more than a celestial problem-solver, Paul entered into the deeper experiences of the Spirit. He anchored his faith in the more significant realities of gratitude, hope, sacrifice, and peace.

Finally, I know Paul is speaking nothing less than God's Word to me because I have found in my own life the truth of these words. Early in the last chapter of Colossians, Paul begins to wind down his letter by returning to the theme of prayer. This is what he said:

> Devote yourselves to prayer, keeping alert in it with thanksgiving. At the same time pray for us as well that God will open to us a door for the word, that we may declare the mystery of Christ, for which I am in prison, so that I may reveal it clearly, as I should. (Col 4:2-4)

I have learned — often through personal difficulty and disappointment — that prayer requires both devotion "to" and alertness "in" its reality. As he began with gratitude, so he reminds the Colossians to always pray "with thanksgiving." Then, shockingly so, Paul asks his Colossian brothers and sisters to pray that he will have opportunity to share his faith in Christ even there in prison. Put yourself in his position. What would you be asking your friends to pray for? If you read these lines carefully, using your imagination and listening with your heart, you will glimpse a Christian life in which fear and anxiety have been transformed into courage and confidence. Living in the deeper reality of prayer, knowing life is "in Christ" and moving toward Christ, freed Paul's life, sustained as it was by faith, love, and hope.

All of us long for that kind of confidence. We rightly ask: Where can I find such serenity, hope, confidence, and peace? Perhaps an ancient prayer would be one place to begin. On the plains of southern England, a community of Christian believers came into existence in the area still referred to by its Latin name Sarum. The Sarum plain of England is the geographical site of ancient circles of monolithic stone and wood, the most famous being Stonehenge. The ancient city of Sarum was the site of a thriving Christian community in the early centuries of the faith. Today, the towering Salisbury cathedral is an enduring witness to the faith of believers in that part of God's world through the ages.

A document that has survived to this day is a worship book we know as the "Sarum Missal." In it, an anonymous believer penned a simple prayer I have committed to memory. Perhaps you would find strength to do the same. Here is what one fellow Christian prayed long ago:

God be in my head and in my understanding;
God be in my eyes and in my looking;
God be in my mouth and in my speaking;
God be in my heart and in my thinking;
God be at my end and at my departing.

The meaning of the prayer, though simple, is profound and beyond any precise definition. At the very least, to know that all our lives are held in the mystery and presence of God brings intentionality and mindfulness to our understanding, our looking, our speaking, our thinking, and our destiny.

You ask, How can prayer become a deeper, more meaningful experience in my life? All of us must ask and answer that question for ourselves. I hear Paul reminding us, through a letter he wrote to believers asking much the same question, to discern a deeper destiny for our spiritual lives than shallow clichés ending with "I hope so." Rather, Paul tells us there is a spring bubbling up with spiritual life and vitality. It's name is hope. It's gifts are faith and love. It's reality is nothing less than the very presence of God in mind, eyes, mouth, heart, and home. Flee prayer's shallow waters where so many drown, desperately clinging to flimsy life preservers. Deep water beckons. Let us pray.

## Prayer

Loving God, teach us to pray. For too long, with too many glib phrases and too few daring words, we have kept you at a safe distance from the lonely caverns of our souls. Teach us to pray.

Teach us to find in you a true friend — someone who listens without prejudice, who affirms without approval, who engages without agenda. Cause us to be more eager to listen for your voice than always to be trying to interpret it. Too often we have given shallow meaning to misunderstood words that both injure our souls and misrepresent your being. Teach us to pray.

Teach us to be more mindful of others in our conversations with you. Remind us that our Lord's model was always *our* rather than *me*, the *Kingdom of God* rather the *country of birth*, *mercy* rather than *money*, *service* rather than *security*. Teach us to pray.

Teach us to long for you so much that we will find strength for life's journey in the secret place and rise gladly to give away ourselves to others in the marketplace. Teach us to pray.

Through the One who taught us to pray, even Jesus our Lord. Amen.

# Notes

[1] I explore the listening side of prayer in my book, *Hearing God in a Noisy World: Prayer as Listening* (Macon: Smyth and Helwys, 1998).

[2] C.F.D. Moule, *The Epistles to the Colossians and Philemon* (The Cambridge Greek New Testament Commentary; Cambridge: Cambridge University Press, 1957), 49.

# Insiders and Outsiders

She steps down from the bus for her first day of middle school. All of eleven-years-old and barely able to remember her new phone number, Michelle prepares herself for what will surely be her most difficult school day to date. Only three weeks ago, her family moved from their comfortable, familiar home in Glasgow, Kentucky to Dunwoody, Georgia, the tony suburb in northeast Atlanta. Michelle, the baby of the family and only daughter, steps off the bus and into a crowd of other 11-year-old girls. They size her up and down as she looks into the faces of strangers who are nothing like the friends she left behind in bucolic, south central Kentucky. Michelle is afraid, not for her safety but for her soul. Who are these nameless comrades? Will they take her in? Which one or two in the sea of leering faces will become her soul's friends? She wants to disappear, wake up from this nightmare, and be back "home" in Glasgow.

Doug Millsaps has just landed the job of all jobs. Top in his class at a midwest state university, he's taken the first step up that long ladder of success. With an accounting degree and a date to take the CPA exam, Doug is feeling on top of the world professionally, trembling with euphoric anxiety emotionally. It is a big firm with unlimited opportunity. But who will be his mentors? When the newness wears off, to whom will he turn for counsel? Where is the power structure in this conglomerate of accountants, consultants, managers, number crunchers? Doug is an outsider who knows the only way up the ladder is to find a way inside the connective rungs that lead to the top.

We human beings are a curious species. Longing for relationships with others in which to experience community, we often withdraw into private shells of insecurity afraid and lonely. A big part of our struggle has to do with things like family background, personality, self-esteem, genes. But another, slippery side of ourselves longs to be included, accepted, approved by those we deem powerful, influential, important. At any point in our life journey, in almost any situation, we are outsiders longing to be included in the group of well-heeled people inside the company, the neighborhood, the club, the church.

Closer to home, who is "in" and who is "out" have been issues dogging the Christian family from Pentecost's infant cry to this hour. From the first generation of the Church as evidenced by the Jerusalem Council (Acts 15) to more recent gatherings of Roman Catholics at Vatican II and other Christian clans in denominational synods and conventions, the Christian family still wants to know: Who is an insider? Whose theology is deemed "right?" What group, what faction in the church or the denomination will win the day? Sadly, many Christian communities have based their criteria for membership more on cultural traditions and inadequate sociological and psychological models than upon the New Testament witnesses. Even when the Bible has been used, it has been largely abused. The best example in American history, of course, is the way the Bible was used for more than two centuries to justify the institution of slavery.

Closer to where I live, Baptists in particular have used various means to determine whether one is inside or outside the denominational community. As a boy, I remember being "voted in" when I presented myself to the Church for membership. Some Baptist churches still ask, when individuals respond to the public invitation at the conclusion of a service, if a member will "make a motion these persons be received"? Someone in the congregation says "So move." On autopilot, the pastor says, "All those in favor say 'Aye.'" And anybody who has sense says "Aye." "All those opposed?" And there is always silence. No one is turned down for any reason that I know of. Yes, there were stories during the civil rights movement of churches in the South not granting membership to blacks, but those situations, as distasteful as they were, played more for the newspapers than within the four walls of local, predominately white Baptist churches.

As I near 50 years of age, deeply involved in a Christian faith community as pastor–member and as an observer of the American church landscape, this "inside–outside" issue seems far more involved than simply granting local church membership to people who want to join up. Let me narrow the topic even further. Ask yourself the following questions. Who would you not admit to membership in your church and on what basis? Is there any biblical evidence suggesting that an official church roll has anything to do with membership in the Body of Christ? What virtues does Scripture reveal are to characterize believers' lives who claim membership in the Church? These are important questions thinking Christians are asking at the threshold of the third millennium.

To be honest, whole Christian communities are being torn apart by the individual and collective ignorance of many with regard to questions like these. The psycho-social issues of homosexuality, marriage and divorce, abortion, euthanasia, interracial marriage, and the ordination of women to name a few are matters that require honest investigation of Scripture and candid dialogue between believers.

In my judgment, more than a few believers and churches today are drowning in shallow water because the biblical evidence defining church membership, participation, and responsibility have been either ignored, forgotten, rejected, or a combination of all three. In this chapter, we will unpack a number of passages from Paul's Letter to the Colossians in an effort to "profile" these first century Christians. A second move, though more difficult, will require that we deduce from the text a profile of those considered outsiders or threatening to the Colossian community. As in other chapters, we will ask the text probing questions. What virtues did Paul applaud in the lives of his Colossian brothers and sisters? What does the text reveal as being an essential quality of a Christian insider versus an outsider? To these questions and others we may encounter along the way, we now turn.

## Profiling the Colossian Insiders

William J. Bennett has captured many of our minds with his provocative bestseller *The Book of Virtues*. In that book, the former Secretary of

Education has collected dozens of stories, poems, and portions of great literature in order to remind us of the collective human family's heritage of morality and virtue. The book has done well. Obviously, we are hungry to get in touch with something we fear has been lost in our rush toward the new age. Paul's Letter to the Colossians is brimming with Christian virtues the Apostle believed were not only important in the Christian life, but were actually evident in the Christian lives of the Colossian believers. Right now, if you've not yet done so, read through the Letter to the Colossians in one sitting. Using a pencil, underline the qualities or virtues Paul highlights in the text. My reading has uncovered no less than 18 virtues–qualities–characteristics–behaviors — pick your own word — Paul identified as visibly present in the lives of Colossian believers. For our part, we will examine six of Paul's 18 "Virtues." As we do, ask yourself if these characteristics among the Colossians are "insider" qualities you celebrate as a believer.

**Faithfulness**

The first Christian virtue meets us in the opening lines of the Letter. Paul identified the Colossian believers as "faithful brothers and sisters in Christ in Colossae" (Col 1:2). Note the two-fold emphasis on the virtue of faithfulness. A Christian insider is a person who is faithful "in Christ" and in relationship with others. In my judgment, faithfulness is the believer's first and enduring "ability." Let me define what I mean.

A faithful person knows the value of *response-ability*. Responsibility is simply the ability to respond to promises and commitments we make to God and others. Too many shallow water Christians are not only drowning themselves, but leading others to drown with them because they have not translated faithfulness into responsibility.

Faithfulness is also about *account-ability*. The Promise Keeper movement–phenomenon among American males a few years ago had many positive qualities going for it. From my perspective, the requirement that "card carrying" Promise Keepers be involved in an accountability group was high on the list of the movement's strengths. When you think about it, faithfulness without accountability is like attempting to enjoy the benefits of living together without marriage. Yes, there are no doubt the physical and emotional pleasures a man and a woman can share together. What is absent from the blind bliss of such an arrangement is the commitment to live in a covenant where both are accountable not only to each other but to the state. Faithfulness without accountability is, to use a graphic metaphor, spiritual fornication. For Paul, faithfulness rightly found it's home "in Christ" and in community. Accountability is required.

A third, but surely not the last ability captured by faithfulness is *depend-ability*. Any pastor, any church leader, any person in any kind of leadership role anywhere will quickly tell you that verbal faithfulness without physical, active, loyal dependability is almost worthless. Christian believers who exhibit the virtue of faithfulness are people on whom you can depend. They are shoulders to lean on, a sleeve to cry on, an ear that listens, a heart that understands, and most of all, a presence that engages the deeper dimensions of your soul. Faithfulness without dependability is like attempting to satisfy your thirst by drinking bitter water; the taste in your mouth is hardly what you expected when you took a drink. What normally happens under such circumstances is that you spit the water out and look elsewhere for fresh water with which to quench your thirst. Bitter is the taste of brothers and sisters who bubble up with phony faithfulness but who know little of responsibility, accountability, and dependability. Paul praised his Colossian brothers and sisters because they were faithful.

Through the years, I have tried to work with "morning dew" Christians. Like the moisture that condenses on our windows in the morning, these brothers and sisters appear in the fresh "morning" of ministry offering all kinds of support, prayers, piety, promises. But when the coolness of the morning is overtaken by the heat of the day, these right-talking, emotive wonders vanish into the church's ether. Mind you, they mean well, but they have no clue as to the meaning of Christian faithfulness. To be an insider in the Christian movement requires devoted faithfulness to Christ, other believers, and the church.

## Bearing Fruit

Paul identified the second virtue, which he uses twice, to be "bearing fruit" (Col 1:6, 10). In verse 6, he applies the word to the Gospel; in verse 10, the word describes the Colossian believers. The Greek word is the participle *karpophorountes*, a two-word hybrid that suggests reproduction. First applied to the Gospel through the lives of the Colossians (v. 6), Paul then returns to the word to emphasize the fact that the Gospel only comes to life through human personalities and labor. The Gospel was "bearing fruit" (v. 6) because the Colossian believers were "bearing fruit in every good work" (v. 10; cf. Eph 2:8-10).

In creation, God blessed both animals and humankind by commanding them "to be fruitful and multiply" (Gen 1:22, 28). Spiritually, Jesus' parable likened the seed of the Gospel as able to produce a spectacular harvest (Mk 4:3-9). The message seems to be clear; it is God's intention for God's creation that we be persons "bearing fruit" in our lives to the greater glory of God (cf. Rom 7:4). There is little virtue in "consuming" spiritual goods on ourselves. Rather, believers are persons who reject the consumer mentality pervasive in American life and choose the way of self-giving, multiplying our life with Christ in the lives of others.

The present American phenomenon of "church hopping" is a perfect example of this fruit-bearing virtue gone bad. People change churches today about as frequently as they trade automobiles. The reason? "I'm not being 'fed'" — as if the Christian believer is nothing more than a consumer of grain in a larger herd of hungry cattle. Yes, all of us require spiritual food. The model for Christian faith, however, is not the consumer model; we are not "in Christ" to take, eat, and solely satisfy our private, self-centered spiritual hungers. To the contrary, deep water believers are persons "in Christ" who see service, worship, Bible study, and prayer as energizing avenues preparing them to "give out" the grace and love placed in their lives by Christ. "Feeding," important as it is, always and quickly leads to "bearing fruit." Otherwise, as Jesus reminded us, we may be "thrown away" and tossed "into the fire" (John 15:6). Believers "in Christ" are persons "bearing fruit."

**Love in the Spirit**

Paul's personal contact with the Colossian church was through his good friend and the church's pastor Epaphras. It was Epaphras who probably visited Paul in prison and shared with him some of the concerns Paul addressed in the letter. In Colossians 1:8, Paul quickly tells the Colossians that Epaphras' first word to him about their common life was of their "love in the Spirit."

Maturing Christian believers are persons whose love, or *agape*, flows out of the work and presence of the Holy Spirit. The phrase "love in the

Spirit" is probably best translated using those four words. The Greek preposition *en*, however, can also be translated "by," "with," and even "through." Thus, Paul could be praising the believers for their "love by the Spirit, with the Spirit," and "through the Spirit." All four translations of the preposition are appropriate; none weaken or distort Paul's delight that in their lives, *agape* was the life-giving, life-affirming reality manifesting itself through their witness, work, and worship. James D. G. Dunn, in his commentary on Colossians, reminds us that the singular reference to "Spirit" in the whole of Colossians is here in this verse.[1] Could it be that Paul, so impressed by Epaphras' report of the church's devotion to the primary virtue of love, used this early opportunity in the letter to lift up *agape* as *the* preeminent virtue in the Christian life? And what of love's presence in our lives?

Someone has said that Paul never got over the inclusive, radical love of God. Met on the Damascus Road as the one who loved him, Jesus Christ pursued Paul with a passion the Apostle never got over. That love was first expressed to him through the arthritic hands of Ananias who was used of God's Spirit to restore Paul's sight. Early in his ministry, God's love affirmed Paul through the ministry of Barnabas, the "son of encouragement." In his writing, Paul lifted up *agape* as the "better way" (1 Cor 13:1), the first "fruit of the Spirit" (Gal 5:22) and the one virtue God expects us to demonstrate both to insiders and outsiders (1 Thess 4:9-12). All this is to say that Paul's devotion to *agape* has it's ultimate foundation in Jesus Christ, who commanded us to "love one another as I have loved you" (John 15:12). So captured by the reality of "love in the Spirit," Paul told the Colossians they were to "clothe" themselves "with love, which binds everything together in perfect harmony" (Col 3:14). Whatever else the Christian church may be, we are never more like our Lord than when we demonstrate radical, affirming, risky "love in the Spirit."

Every Christian struggles with the demands of *agape* love. In all candor, my struggle takes place on the soul's plains between my lips and my hands. My lips say, "God loves all people, period." But my hands war with my lips because I am so afraid to reach out to the homosexual, the AIDS patient, the unwed mother, the adulterous husband. My lips say, "All who know Christ as Lord are my brothers and sisters." But my hands normally reach out to those who intone the Gospel with my words, using my methods, having read books from my approved list. The struggle is an all out war. For believers, "Love in the Spirit" becomes real love when our hearts summon our hands to act in love and they obey. The writer of James wrote, "Faith without works is dead." Paul is saying, "Love without works is phony."

## Gratitude

Of all the virtues Paul commends to the Colossians, the virtue of gratitude is mentioned more than any other. And how could it not be? Paul's opening line in the Letter, as found in the Greek text, begins by saying "We thank God" (Col 1:3). Paul saw in the Colossians a virtue he found relentlessly flowing through his life. Get the picture. Here is a person hell-bent on destroying the Christian faith only to discover the very One he was seeking to destroy is the same One who pursues him in love. Anyone who has ever experienced anything close to that kind of undeserved, unbridled, forgiving love knows of only one response: Thank you.

So it is in the Christian life. Gratitude is to be as natural to our lifestyle, speech, and behavior as seeing is to the gift of vision. So radical is Christian gratitude, that Paul admonished the Colossians, even when faced with persecution, to give thanks "to the Father" (Col 1:12). In fact, according to Paul, we are to be a people both individually and collectively "abounding in thanksgiving" (Col 2:7). Gratitude is such a significant reality in the life of the Christian, that it is dynamically linked to the much sought after gift of "peace" (Col 3:15) and the experience of corporate worship (Col 3:17). "Giving thanks to God," or the "Eucharist," is the worship experience in which we discover we are most connected to God. So central is this idea to Roman Catholicism, that Catholic believers understand the bread and wine of the Mass actually become the body and blood of Christ. Gratitude "feeds" our lives with spiritual food, empowering us to be as Christ to others.

Too many Christian believers today, infected with the "me first" mentality of contemporary consumer society, have missed the joy of giving in all its varied and affirming dimensions. The virtue of gratitude, according to Colossians, is far more than the mumbling of "thank you" for kindnesses done for us. Gratitude, as Christian virtue, is the living out of our lives in response to the grace and love of God. In Christ, we are to be persons in whose lives the giving of our financial resources, our time in Christian service, our lives in transformational worship and prayer, and the sacrifice of our pride in being present to others is always a "what more can I do" response to God. Gratitude is not the concluding response to God's grace, but rather the beginning.

**Buried and Raised with Christ**

The fourth in our series of six distinctive virtues is no virtue at all to those outside of the Christian experience. Paul, in two places in Colossians, reminds us that Christian believers are persons who have been buried and raised with Christ (Col 2:12-13; 3:1-4). How is this spiritual reality a "virtue" of insiders in the Christian family? Put simply, believers are individuals who now carry in their bodies, their lives, their experience, a cross and an empty tomb. Insiders are persons who are very human, but who nevertheless have become children of God through the death and resurrection of Jesus Christ.

This reality in the Christian life is best illustrated through the very physical experience of Christian baptism. In the Baptist tradition, baptism is a bodily experience in which one who has placed his or her faith in Jesus Christ is immersed in water in the Name of the Father, the Son, and the Holy Spirit. Baptism outwardly pictures one's inward commitment to Jesus Christ, crucified, buried, and risen. Paul beautifully described this spiritual reality in the sixth chapter of his Letter to the Romans (Rom 6:1-11). Simply stated, baptism is the outward expression of an inward change. Water, long associated with death in Hebrew thought, becomes the physical picture of our death with Christ. Once placed under death's reality, we rise to "new life" in Christ by his resurrection from death.

Christian insiders are persons who live conscious of the fact that baptismal water will always drip off of our brows. This same reality was expressed by Paul when he reminded the Corinthians, "For while we live, we are always being given up to death for Jesus' sake, so that the life of Jesus may be made visible in our mortal flesh. So death is at work in us, but life in you" (2 Cor 4:11-12). What does this mean? At the very least, it means that Christian believers are persons who have "died" to self-centeredness and who are spiritually alive for others. We are persons who know sin destroys, wounds, and kills. Freed by the power of Christ's life from the selfish, destructive power of sin that seeks only to save the self, believers "live" for others "in Christ." If you have said, "Jesus Christ is Lord," you are a person who is "buried and raised with Christ." Insiders are those who are dead, yet alive in Christ.

**Internally Disciplined**

One of the challenges facing the Colossian believers was an apparent intrusion into their lives of external, albeit spiritual requirements from some outside source. Unlike the Galatian situation, where believers had actually abandoned their simple faith in Christ for an oppressive legalism (Gal 1:6-9), the Colossians seemed to be juggling suggestions from outsiders that could "improve" their Christian faith (Col 2:20-23). Paul, using first century concepts, tied such "extra" ideas to those which had been abandoned when the Colossians first believed in Christ. Unable or unprepared to accept the simple, but profound reality of living in faith, outsiders had told the Colossians they needed to add several important "regulations" to their lifestyle. "Do not handle, Do not taste, Do not touch" sounds like prohibitions one would speak to a two year old. Words like control, immaturity, childish come to mind when I read these verses.

What is Paul saying? He seems to be teaching the Colossians that believers "in Christ" are persons who are internally disciplined. In fact, he concludes this brief section of the Letter by reminding them that all external rules, regulations, and laws have "no value in checking self-indulgence" (Col 2:23). Every adult knows this to be true. All the laws passed by Congress, the law enforcement officials employed, and prisons built cannot change the heart of humankind. Only God can do that. In fact, maturity of life and soul is such an "inside" job, that believers are called to find "within" the resources to live "without." Christian insiders are self-disciplined. Legalism, judgmental attitudes, or some arbitrary list of "Dos and Don'ts" all together cannot change the human heart and will.

Here is the folly of all creeds, insider theological checklists, and positional votes by denominational bodies. To be internally disciplined is to know that outside pressure is not the method God uses to change any human mind, action, or idea. God's Spirit works on the inside of believers motivating them to believe and act "in Christ." We who comprise the Christian family would be wise to go to school on Paul's provocative corrective. Baptists and other free church believers have always insisted on the central role of conscience in shaping one's theology and behavior. Church history tells us adopting creeds, signing statements of faith, excluding all who don't agree with us never advances the Kingdom of God. To be internally disciplined is to be ruled by the Spirit, not some temporary creed constructed by fallible human beings.

**Partners, not Competitors, in God's work**

Finally, Christian insiders see others within the family of faith as partners, not competitors. Colossians 4:7-17 is a very personal communiqué from Paul to the Colossians where he mentions ten men and women who were partners with him in his ministry. Some were prisoners with him — Aristarchus and Jesus-Justus. Others may have been frequent guests who encouraged Paul — Luke and Demas. Reading these eleven verses, apart from the situations raised in the lives of these men and women, gives one the clear impression that Paul's companions were devoted to each other. Did they differ on matters of theology? We know that Mark and Paul actually separated for a time because of some personal dispute, but that misunderstanding did not turn them into Christian competitors. Did these ten people express their faith in Christ in lock-step uniformity? I doubt it. In fact, Paul indicates that at least three of his friends — Aristarchus, Mark, and Jesus-Justus — were Jewish Christian believers. We know from Acts that Jewish Christians worshiped in the Temple, something a Gentile believer would not have been able to do.

Candor requires me to note that the infant Christian movement dealt with the competitive nature of humankind early on. This surfaced, for example, in the Jew-Gentile controversy already alluded to at the beginning of the chapter. Acts 15 records the key events surrounding the Jerusalem Council at which Paul appealed to church leaders to accept Gentiles who had turned in faith to Christ. Though the chief effect of that Council was to steer the infant Church in a more inclusive, non-legalistic direction, the long-term implications of the Council's decisions are still being sorted out in contemporary church history.

Even so, the profile captured from these personal lines from Paul about his friends indicates a partnership in ministry not a competition for status or power. Contemporary believers would be wise to learn from the early church. To our shame, too many Christians are suspicious of each other, rather than implementing the New Testament admonition to encourage each other. Churches competing with other churches for members — rightly called "sheep" stealing — neither honors God nor advances the Christian faith. Catholics suspicious of Baptists, Methodists critiquing the work of Pentecostals, and so forth cripples the common witness of Christian believers to the One who prayed that all who followed him might be one (John 17:20-21).

Christian insiders have much to celebrate in the lives of fellow believers. God calls us to be faithful in our witness to Christ and vigilant in guarding each other's reputation. I have made a covenant I ask you to join me in. I will speak no demeaning, critical words against any brother or sister on whose lips and in whose life Jesus is Lord. If Jesus were speaking to us, I believe he would take that one step further. Jesus would urge us to speak only that which blesses and strengthens others. Such speech is always "gracious" and in keeping with the Spirit of the risen Lord (Col 4:6).

What picture does the Letter to the Colossians give us of Christian insiders? To the six Christian virtues I have listed above, Paul reveals that believers are persons who are reconciled to God (Col 1:21-22), holy, blameless, and irreproachable (Col 1:22-23), guardians of the mystery (Col 1:25-27), rescued from death (Col 1:13), living in the peace of Christ (Col 3:15), committed to being a community of worship in Christ (Col 3:16-17), respecting relationships within family (Col 3:18–4:1), and are deeply involved in the life of prayer (Col 4:2-4). A much shorter list awaits our study as we now look at Paul's surprising profile of outsiders.

## Profiling the Colossian Outsiders

You would think, would you not, that Paul would have a number of indicators in the Colossian letter profiling those who opposed the Christian faith in that ancient city. I was surprised to discover only three characteristics of a Colossian outsider. Like the positive profile of insiders above, this brief list attempts to pull out of the text words and concepts Paul deemed as dangerous or threatening to the Christian faith. Let's take a look.

## Deceptive

Colossians 2:4 is a warning to the insiders to beware of people who may "deceive you with plausible arguments." I find it extremely provocative that Paul's word here translated "deceive" is the Greek word whose literal meaning is "coming alongside speech." People who are deceptive are individuals who know the right language, but who use language to subvert or outright attack others. In a Christian context, deceptive people do not reveal the whole story about themselves: they play at relationships rather than invest in them, use words to divide people rather than unite them, and show up in the church to confuse and disturb the fellowship rather than being in the community, shaping and serving with the community.

Deceptive "outsiders" may or may not be church members. In my experience, some of the most destructive people I have known in my life are "card carrying" members of the church.[2] For reasons not even known to their psychiatrist, deceptive people use others within the church to further their own agendas. The church becomes the place and God's people become the community where unresolved anger, disappointment, and grief are dumped on unsuspecting brothers and sisters.

This was apparently the case at Colossae. Paul never indicates that the "outsiders" were hostile, adversarial, belligerent, or combative persons physically "outside" the church fellowship. Most scholars see a situation radically different from Galatians where Judaizers were cajoling Christian believers to abandon the "salvation by grace through faith" Gospel for a religion of faith plus Jewish legalism. Here, the Colossians seem to be dealing primarily with an internal challenge, all the while seeking to find their unity and purpose under the Lordship of Christ. Perhaps they did not even know they were doing it, but the Colossian "outsiders" were relating to the rest of the Church in deceptive and destructive ways.

## Christ-less

A second characteristic of the Colossian outsiders was their Christ-less attitude (Col 2:8). In my judgment, it's entirely possibly to consider oneself a Christian and yet have little understanding or awareness of the One whose name we have taken. To be "in Christ" means, at the very least, to be a follower of Jesus Christ; to embrace his values, his way of relating to others, his sacrificial behavior, his self-less giving. Outsiders, even though they consider themselves Christian, are persons who are more self than Christ. In the church, this is often seen in the political hassles every church experiences from time to time. This group likes the minister, another group cannot stand the minister, and the vast majority in the middle simply want peace. Where is Christ? One group thinks the largest portion of the church's resources ought to be given away to missions, another group believes missions requires direct involvement by members, and a third sees missions as something others do entirely. Where is Jesus?

Christ-less outsiders, like their deceptive cousins, may be very involved in the life of a local congregation. They may even be decision-makers on church governing bodies, but they have little interest in the life of the Spirit, personal and corporate worship, Bible study, involvement in ministry or missions, and so forth. They may make compelling speeches, know exactly what meetings to attend and who to shmooze with, but they have little personal, intimate knowledge of Christ. Christian outsiders are Christ-less.

**Judgmental**

Finally, Paul tells us Christian outsiders are judgmental (Col 2:16-19). Be careful here. Paul is not saying Christians outsiders use poor judgment. All of us do that from time to time. It's a defect in our human engineering; we are fallible creatures. What Paul is saying is that outsiders to the community of faith are persons who define who they are by what others do and believe, don't do or don't believe, or by how others behave or practice their faith. In a lengthy list of primarily religious behaviors, Paul revealed that certain individuals were sitting in judgment on persons who did not have the same religious experiences or exhibit the same religious behaviors as "they" did.

Rather than being judgmental, believers are called to be faithful to the Lord Jesus Christ who alone is judge over all humankind and human behavior. That is not to say we must jettison sound judgment when weighing the merits of certain practices or behaviors. Paul's admonition to "the strong" about "the weak" in Romans 14:1-23 is teaching from which we all would profit if we read it more often. Let it be enough to say here that Christian "outsiders" have taken God's place on the judgment seat of eternity; they have put themselves in the place of God.

# Insiders...Outsiders

So what of this conversation about insiders and outsiders? What have we learned by profiling this ancient Christian community? In a comprehensive way, the unity of the church is the purpose of Paul's entire letter. Read the four chapters carefully and you get this overwhelming picture of a person struggling to keep the Christian community united around one head, even Christ. So who is an insider? In a word, an insider is one who is a disciple of Jesus Christ. Insiders are following — feel the active, dynamic quality of that word — Jesus. On the other hand, what makes a Christian "outsider"? Outsiders are out-to-lunch when it comes to the church's primary purpose and mission. Outsiders are more concerned with getting their way than discovering in community God's leadership and direction. Outsiders often have a hidden agenda while thinking no one knows what that is, when in fact the majority of "insiders" do know. Outsiders think they are "in" when in fact they are marginalized and politely ignored.

Paul sounds a clear warning to all of us who, from time to time, are in danger of drowning in shallow water. Yes, there are virtues which are born and move toward maturity in the lives of Christian believers. To live out the virtues of gratitude, fruit bearing, love, and so forth is risky and demanding. To be a Christian, in the words of my beloved mentor Dr. Frank Stagg, is both gift and demand. Insiders choose to mature following the difficult and demanding, but highly rewarding way revealed in Jesus Christ. Insiders are following Jesus. Yes, it's risky. But the alternative is a shallow water drowning.

Profiling the individual believer from the text of Colossians is a helpful and rewarding study. In doing so, I have deliberately left off Paul's profile of the new community in Colossians 3:5-17. To that provocative text we now turn in the next chapter.

# Prayer

Including and affirming God, you love the world so much you want every human being and all creation to be in fellowship with you. Where we divide the human family by race, nationality, geography, education, gender, power, you alone call us to come together around the one person who gave his life for us all, even Jesus Christ.

Forgive us for narrow thinking and even more narrow living, for keeping people at a safe, manageable distance where we decide who is in and who is out. We confess that when all our sorting is done, we are still lonely and afraid and so very distant from the inclusive, grace-giving love of Jesus.

God of all creation, teach us to be so mentally and spiritually disciplined, so relationally open, that we will receive others as you have received us. Erase from the hard drive of our minds all color-coding and gender-qualifying programs and in their place, install and run the overwhelming operating system of your grace.

May your Kingdom come and your will be done on earth as it is in heaven. Through Jesus Christ, who takes us in, we pray. Amen.

# Notes

[1] James D.G. Dunn, *The Epistles to the Colossians and to Philemon* (Grand Rapids: Wm. B. Eerdmans Publishing, 1996), 66.

[2] Here is a classic "Catch-22." Persons who need the Church to be the redemptive, healing, accepting People of God are often those who cannot or will not name the pain in their lives. Instead, they work out their own pain through destructive behaviors within the church. I learned long ago from one of my mentors that a person who is "acting out" at church — verbally abusive, critical, negative, fault-finding — is often a person in whose life is some great sorrow, failure, sin that cannot be named, faced, forgiven, and forsaken. More times than not, church members who are constantly critical or negative need our prayers and the healing work of God's Spirit.

# The New Community

An older couple, both widowed, began dating each other, nervously trying to decide whether marriage was the right thing. Their adult children seemed okay with the relationship; friends were encouraging. Finally, the guy popped the question over candlelight and roses to which his lady said, "I'll marry you provided you understand Tippy (her beloved poodle) comes with the marriage." They married — man, woman, dog — and lived "happily ever after." "They" became family along with their adult children, sons and daughters-in-law, grandchildren, extended family, and a trainload of memories.

All of us who are married know that when you wed the person of your dreams, he or she comes with an entourage of family, friends, habits, sometimes pets, and much more. We marry a person — an individual — and that person's network of relationships and experiences. Marriage is a "total package" arrangement that is inescapable and incredibly nurturing. That this is so ought be no overwhelming revelation. When it is good, a marriage relationship is mutually nourishing, uncommonly empowering, at times overwhelmingly joyful.

Something else is at work in the human experience that is mirrored in marriage; something far more inclusive, connected, communal. Each of us is far more than an independent, isolated self. The rugged individuality so praised in American folklore is precisely that: lore. Each one of us is an individual, yet we are inextricably woven together with other individuals in the complex fabric of life. From the moment human beings first walked on planet Earth, we have sought and needed each other. The uniqueness of our fingerprints only seems to intensify the longing for others with whom to grasp fingers, join hands, embrace, talk, work, create. We are not fully human individually without being human in community.

The Christian faith brashly believes, without apology, that our best individuality and finest expression of community is possible through our common faith in Jesus Christ. The Christian experience is fiercely personal and radically corporate.[1] In fact, the New Testament never recognizes or even hints at the possibility of a personal relationship with Jesus Christ as Lord apart from the larger, community experience in the Church. In Christ, we are spiritually, physically, relationally, purposefully woven into the lives of other believers. My faith in Christ as Lord is only "Christian" to the degree I live out my confession of faith with brothers and sisters with whom I share it.

Kathleen Norris, in her delightful and nourishing book *The Cloister Walk*, takes us with her into a Benedictine convent, there to experience the life of worship and community over the span of several months. Reared in the Protestant tradition, Norris learned much from her Roman Catholic sisters. "For myself, I have found that being a member of a church congregation, and also following, as I am able, the discipline of Benedict's Rule, has helped me to take my path toward God without falling into the trap of thinking of myself as 'a church of one.'"[2] Others are one of God's gifts to us, reaching out their hands and hearts to bring our individual relationship to Christ into some community expression.

The Bible calls this individual–corporate reality "the new community" through faith in Jesus as Lord. In Jesus Christ, we discover both our true selves as loved, forgiven, and wanted by God and our brothers and sisters who have also experienced God's work in their lives. The New Testament refers to the new community by using strong and evocative language: "Body of Christ," "People of God," "fellowship," "church," "people of the Way," "saints," and even "synagogue" are but a few of the words expressing this profoundly nourishing reality we call the Church.

Of course, by now you know I detect a shallow water situation in which many believers today are drowning. And you are right. I decided to write this chapter on the new community near the end of the book for two reasons: (1) I believe there is more ignorance today than ever before on the nature and purpose of the Church; and (2) only a careful reading of Scripture can summon us to build our communities of faith on New Testament models. As before, I ask you to join me in resisting the temptation to formulate a rigid theology of the Church, lists of "rights" and "rules," or narrow definitions which inhibit a particular community of faith from expressing its life in Christ in the culture and situation where God has placed it. The first century churches in Colossae and Jerusalem could not have been more different; the former strongly Gentile, the latter strongly Jewish. Diversity elbows its way out of the New Testament in spite of every attempt we make to speak of *the* New Testament Church. With that in mind, let's listen as Paul talks about the Church as revealed in the Letter to the Colossians.

## Community "In Christ"

Paul's Colossian letter opens a window into the new community "in Christ" in Colossae. In the last chapter, we profiled the Christian believer. In the pages that follow, I invite you to look with me at thirteen verses from Colossians that give us a glimpse of the kind of new community in which the Gospel of Christ lives, multiplies, and thrives. In my judgment, the church in the new millennium has much to anticipate and celebrate as it builds its common life on these first century principles. In so doing, we become partners with God in protecting ourselves from drowning in the shallow waters of surface relationships in the place we call our church home. What makes a collection of human beings a community of faith? What does it mean to be a Church, the people of God, in the third millennium of the Christian movement? Let's find out.

### A Transforming Community

> Put to death, therefore, whatever in you is earthly: fornication, impurity, passion, evil desire, and greed (which is idolatry). On account of these the wrath of God is coming on those who are disobedient. These are the ways you also once followed, when you were living that life. But now you must get rid of all such things — anger, wrath, malice, slander, and abusive language from your mouth. Do not lie to one another, seeing that you have stripped off the old self with its practices and have

clothed yourselves with the new self, which is being renewed in knowledge according to the image of its creator. (Col 3:5-10)

These lines almost slap us in the face or worse, burn our ears, tuned as they are to the strict, puritanical teaching of our ancestors. Colossians 3:5-10 records a list of vices Christians are to "put to death" in our lives. "Fornication, impurity, passion, evil desire, and greed" are to have no place in the new community. Likewise, Paul goes on to list "anger, wrath, malice, slander, and abusive language" along with lying as being equally offensive to God. Let's put these two lists together.

The first list — fornication, impurity, passion, evil desire, and greed — are five sins Peter T. O'Brien notes "were vices for which the Jews especially reproached the pagans."[3] Clearly, Paul told the Colossians these particular vices were "ways you once followed" before turning to Christ (Col 3:7). I find it especially significant that the list begins with fornication (prostitution, sexual immorality) and ends with greed (insatiable acquiring, consuming) which, parenthetically, Paul calls "idolatry." When you think about it, sexual immorality is a form of greed. In fact, in our society, consumer sex is as easy to secure as a line of credit; you can phone for it, read it, view it, buy it, and use it to your heart's satisfaction if you choose.

Likewise, we are a greedy people, consuming so much beyond our own ability to pay for it. Our enormous national debt is only a monstrous reflection of private consumer debt plaguing so many household budgets today. In both situations — sexual immorality and greed — the operative, controlling, could I say foundational sin is idolatry. Any time we worship an appetite, whether it's sex, drugs, alcohol, gambling, food, even shopping, we turn what God calls "holy" into something ugly and destructive. According to the Hebrew Scriptures, idolatry was the first and most sinister of all temptations. The first two of the Ten Commandments clearly tell us so (cf. Ex 20:3-6).

Note something else in this text. Between "fornication" and "greed" are three other vices: impurity, passion, and evil desire. Scholars are in agreement that Paul's list of vices tumbles out of a culture where pagan ritual was often associated with sexual activity.[4] That said, Paul may have observed another danger posed to believers: a subtle but deadly drifting back into the idolatry from which many of these early believers came. Granted, more than a few of the Colossian believers may have come to faith in Christ out of Judaism (cf. Col 2:8-14a). That possibility notwithstanding, the reality remains: sexual immorality, idolatry, and greed rear their destructive heads in lives where impurity, unbridled passion, and evil desire are controlling the heart and will. Paul commands the Colossians to "Put to death," execute without delay, these deadly, destructive, and dehumanizing behaviors. Put another way, these enemies of faith cannot be appeased; we must kill them, and quickly. So Paul commands the Colossians to execute promptly these demanding, greedy "gods." He does not say, "You have *already* put to death" these sins. Rather, he says at the time he writes, "Put these sins to death *now*" (emphasis mine). Paul is writing to Christian believers who still struggle with temptation, sin, failure, immorality, guilt.

Here is a helpful word to the contemporary church. These deadly sins, if not killed, will kill us and those with whom we share the life of faith. Becoming a transforming community takes time and generous amounts of grace. Rather than being the community of the convinced, the comfortable, the perfect, the all-together, the Church is a community continually being transformed by Christ's presence in our midst. This is an ongoing, focused process helped by simply being together as God's people in worship, Bible study, prayer, and service to others. A wise fellow pastor tells the people who join the Church where he serves that if they will simply "show up" for Bible study, worship, and times of fellowship, they will "catch" much of the spirit and power of being a Christian. This happens because the Church is a transforming community of believers.

How is that possible? Quite frankly, if you are talking about individual effort, you are looking near defeat in the eye. Missing in our English translations is Paul's consistent use of second person plural nouns and verbs in his writing. The text of Colossians 3:5-10 has no less than three "you" pronouns in the plural: "*You* put to death," "But now *you* must get rid of all such things," and "*You* do not lie." In the deep South, we say "y'all." Paul called the entire Christian community to be involved in actualizing the transforming power of the Gospel.

We all of us know at some level that authentic personal transformation cannot take place without the involvement of others. Alcoholics Anonymous has taught us that some behaviors cannot be "put to death" without the support of a caring, nonjudgmental, and confidential community. In Jesus Christ, God forms the new community as a transforming interconnection of human lives so linked to God and each other that phony "God substitutes" are both named and rejected for the impostors they are. The Church is a transforming community because in its embrace, we refuse to "bow down" to the idols of sexual promiscuity and greed, so prominent in every era. In practice, any God-rejecting way of life, "the ways you also once followed," must continually be faced, named, and shunned by followers of Jesus Christ. The new community's devotion solely belongs to God.

How tempted we are at every turn to displace our loyalty to God with God-substitutes, many of which are quite respectable. An example would be placing our lives in faith's hands, rather than God's. The popular phrases, "I believe" and "Have faith" have a ring of authenticity until you ask "Believe who?" and "Have faith in what?" Many today believe their feelings, the media, popular sentiment about morality, or politically correct positions on biblically questionable practices. At every turn along life's way, our summons is to follow God as revealed in Jesus Christ. Only God is worthy of our worship and able to sustain our lives.

Next, Paul turns his attention from the temptations inherent in sexual immorality and idolatry to the less obvious sins needing to be named in the Colossian fellowship. Apparently, the Colossian Christians were having difficulty with the pesky, very human imperfections found in anger, wrath, malice, slander, abusive language, and lying — sins that all interface in some way with the mouth! I don't know about you, but the gnawing, destructive sin in my life has less to do with "fornication" and "greed" as it does this flapping muscle in my head better known as the tongue. Paul makes it plain later on: "Let your speech always be gracious, seasoned with salt, so that you may know how you ought to answer everyone" (Col 4:6). The message from both lists Paul gives us is plain: members of God's new community must name, forsake, and refuse to compromise with sin. Why? Because sin destroys lives and distorts reality.

Make no mistake about it, sin is not dead or quietly waiting to die in any life. Though we have been buried and raised with Christ, we still wrestle with the last gasping, flailing, dangerous reality of sin. Paul uses the same "buried and risen" imagery in speaking directly to the Colossians about sin. "You have stripped off the old self with its practices and have clothed yourselves with the new self, which is being renewed in knowledge according to the image of its creator" (Col 3:9-10). Notice the words "being renewed." The English phrase translates the one Greek participle *anakainoumenon*. The present tense participle carries the idea of that which is continually ongoing. Insiders deal openly and honestly with sin because they know that God's Spirit is continually renewing, making new those who have committed their lives to Christ.

Here is a very personal illustration of this truth. I am solidly and irrevocably in love with Kathie, my wife of over 26 years. In fact, whatever definition I used to have of love is now of no use to me because her faithfulness and devotion to me has redefined whatever it was I used to think love was. To my own loss and sorrow, however, I don't always express to her the same degree of love and trust she expresses to me. Even so, her love is continually beckoning me to be more than I am through the power of the love she and God pour into my life. And yes, when I hurt or disappoint her, I must deal openly and honestly with her because I love her more than I love my hurtful behavior. In profound and personal ways, members of the new community individually and collectively express the fact that we are "in love" with Jesus Christ. His faithfulness to us is continually making us new to the degree we choose love over selfishness, grace over greed, and hope over despair.

Contrary to the teaching of some spiritual gurus in this new age, spirituality cannot be glimpsed, much less experienced, looking in the shiny mirror of individuality. To become a "Jesus" person requires participation in the new community being transformed by Jesus' power and life. The shallow waters of individualistic feelings are a poor substitute for the fuller experience of communal life, where the transforming grace of God comes to us through many voices, stories, memories, and hopes.

Christian believers are struggling today with society's unrelenting summons to individual freedom. One of the great ironies of this age is our insistent longing for doing it "my way" even as we fight the perennial human realities of isolation, loneliness, and meaning. The new community in Jesus Christ is transforming to the degree we express and understand our individuality within the embrace of a forgiving, grace-giving, accountable body of believers.

Through my years of ministry, I have both experienced personally and witnessed in the lives of brothers and sisters in Christ such radical acceptance in the embrace of the Church. God's grace, demonstrated in community, so frees individuals to become who God created them to be that selfishness is transformed into sacrifice, fear into courage, despair into hope, and bitterness into life. But there is more at work in this new community in Christ.

### An Inclusive Community

> In that renewal there is no longer Greek and Jew, circumcised and uncircumcised, barbarian, Scythian, slave and free; but Christ is all and in all! (Col 3:11)

Paul now summons the entire church to see something so radical and yet so distinctive about the Christian faith as to explode all first century notions of what it means to live with others in the human community, much less the new community God has inaugurated in Jesus Christ. I wonder if we, with third millennium ears, can hear what God communicated through God's servant Paul?

Having told the Colossians they are being made new "in the image" of the One who created them, Paul now tells them the consequences of God's renewing work: there are to be no human-made distinctions between persons, ever. The new community is to be an inclusive community where all persons are accepted as persons, period. Again, James D. G. Dunn adds an insight gathered from the tiny conjunction "and" in the text. "Greek *and* Jew, circumcised *and* uncircumcised, barbarian, Scythian, slave *and* free." The "and" is "the way of categorizing humankind into two classes."[5] Using language, we classify people into controllable groupings: whites and blacks, Hispanics and Europeans, saved and lost. It's a very convenient and sometimes destructive use of an innocent conjunction.

I grew up believing there were Americans *and* everyone else in the world. In fact, during the frothy moments of the Cuban missile crisis in the early 60s, I remember looking at a map of the world, trying to decide who would line up with "us" against the heathen Russians. "And" is a powerful controller in our vocabulary. Paul says insiders must be on their guard, knowing that the classifying of human beings quickly devolves into rules and laws that control who's acceptable *and* who's not.

This obvious classification–controlling tendency within the human species identified by Paul has implications in other areas of human life. Where Paul uses racial, religious, and political definitions, others surely would apply, as he so notes in his letter to the Galatians (3:28). Specifically, Paul addressed the "male–female" distinction in his warning to the Galatians. Like the racial, religious, and political classifications we readily use to control our relationships with others, so too gender is a powerful classifier-–controller. Today, as in no other era of human history, the Christian community must be a place where both men and women are empowered to actualize their full devotion and service to Jesus Christ. With secularity, materialism, and fear still hunting and haunting the human family, the Christian community must model the Gospel ideal that we are all "one in Christ" (Gal 3:28) and that "Christ is all, and in all" (Col 3:11). The new community is an inclusive fellowship where all human identities are eclipsed by God's naming us God's children. In a world where hyphenation (African-American, Anglo-Catholic, inner city youth) is on the rise, the Christian community simplifies life by saying we are "one" in Christ: no "ands," no hyphens, no barriers.

Difficult issues, however, face the inclusive new community that require an honest response in the Spirit of Christ. The church's relationship to homosexuals is one such issue. Will homosexuals be excluded from participation in the life of the Church? For most congregations, the issue of gay and lesbian ordination to ministry is not a significant, life or death matter. The tradition in which I minister and my own convictions about homosexuality prohibit me from participating in the ordination of a homosexual. My reasons are primarily scriptural. In my judgment, the Bible clearly names homosexual behavior as being inconsistent with God's intention for humankind. Saying that homosexuality is not God's intention for men or women, however, in no way condemns or stands in judgment of homosexuals.

Theologically, the distinction between the sin and the sinner is clear: alcoholism is deadly, but the alcoholic is beloved of God; prostitution is immoral, but the prostitute is beloved of God; child abuse is both evil and destructive, but the child abuser and abused are beloved of God. Faith's insiders are persons who accept with God's love the sinner while refusing to condone or call acceptable the sin. The inclusive community of faith invites all to experience the transforming grace of God; a grace that heals, frees, empowers the life by faith.

A good friend met me for breakfast more than a year ago. As we sat across the table, I sensed our conversation was going to take a profoundly personal, possibly painful turn. Without saying the "h" word, we talked about being actively involved in our fellowship. My friend is gay. My role as pastor was not to sit in judgment on his life, but to sit in grace before his life. He knew where I stand on homosexuality; he also knows where I stand on being his brother in Christ. Was it easy? No. The hard work of grace is never easy, but it is always renewing. Our relationship as friends, my role as pastor, his willingness to talk and our commitment to Christ still calls me to be faithful to him without being disloyal to my conscience or my convictions.

Isn't this what we observe in Jesus' relationships with individuals as recorded in the four Gospels? At every turn, our Lord "ate with tax collectors (the hated ones) and sinners (the outcast ones)." He broke all social conventions while radically fulfilling the Law of God. Jesus included all kinds of rule breakers in his company; lepers, prostitutes, the lame, the blind, outcasts, the hungry. In so doing, Jesus shows us that being strong on including all in no way means being weak in upholding righteousness. The very fact "sinners" responded to Jesus gives witness to their awareness that something in their lives was missing only the accepting love of God could fill; something was wrong only God could make right; something was lost only God could find. The new community following Jesus Christ fulfills God's mission to the degree it demonstrates God's inclusive love.

**A Compassionate Community**

> As God's chosen ones, holy and beloved, clothe yourselves with compassion, kindness, humility, meekness, and patience. Bear with one another and, if anyone has a complaint against another, forgive each other; just as the Lord has forgiven you, so you also must forgive. Above all, clothe yourselves with love, which binds everything together in perfect harmony. And let the peace of Christ rule in your hearts, to which indeed you were called in one body. (Col 3:12-15a)

The new community in Christ is a transforming, inclusive community whose common life bears witness to the compassion of Jesus. Here, Paul commands the Colossians to clothe themselves with the risky gifts of "compassion, kindness, humility, meekness, and patience" (Col 3:12). You may not have thought about it in these terms, but caring for others as Christ cares for us is indeed risky business. Take a moment and reflect upon the pain being endured by human beings, animals, the earth, indeed all creation at this very moment in history. I believe you will agree with me that not a one of those bleeding situations is finding much help or hope in the confines of laws, resolutions, or speeches. The opposite is true. In fact, every bleeding, hurting place and person on this planet could be immeasurably helped by receiving genuine compassion, kindness, humility, meekness, and patience.

These gifts–virtues were personified in our Lord. Jesus "went about doing good." His life was one in which virtuous words became enfleshed in holy hands. Jesus did more than talk a good line; he acted on behalf of others and in so doing, through his death on the cross, the human family receives the opportunity to experience life with a capital "L." The new community is a fellowship of persons whose very lives are "clothed" with Jesus' life. Isn't this what Paul meant when, a few verses earlier, he wrote "[you] have clothed yourselves with the new self." Paul told the Corinthians as much when he wrote, "If anyone is in Christ, he or she is a new creation" (2 Cor 5:17). To be "in Christ," is to be a new creation, a new species, a recreated human being, if you please, clothed with the character of Jesus. What does that mean? At the very least it means that when you and I get to the place in life — as we all surely do — where choices must be made about values, character, integrity, and compassion, we are wise to remember this: Do what Jesus would do and we will do not only the right thing, but the loving and compassionate thing.

The five virtues Paul lists in these verses — compassion, kindness, humility, meekness, and patience — are similar to other lists of virtues Paul included in his letters to the Galatians (5:22-23) and the Ephesians (4:1-2). I find it intriguing that many scholars believe that of the letters of Paul we have in our New Testament, Galatians may be the first letter Paul wrote and Ephesians may have been his last letter. Thus, from his first to his last letter and obviously one in between, Colossians, Paul could not escape the reality of the new community in which believers live. Notice Paul used a word translated here as "chosen ones." The Greek word is *eklektos*, from which the English word "elect" finds its origin. C.F.D. Moule argues convincingly that Paul's use of this word and it's cousins, "election" and "the called," drive home the sweeping revelation that the new community in Christ is God's New Israel (cf. 1 Thess 1:4).[6]

Unlike Judaism, what sets God's people apart "in Christ" is no longer circumcision, faithfulness to kosher laws, or obedience to the Law, but rather the outward demonstration in community of nothing less than the very life of Christ. The Church is "the Body of Christ."

Notice too that part of compassion's work among us is the need to "bear with one another." The New Revised Standard Version quoted above does the Greek text a disservice by separating the phrases "bear with one another" and "forgive each other." The Greek text has the first phrase followed directly by the second. The phrases are actually translations of two present participles used with the force of imperatives. A more literal reading of the text is: "Bearing with one another and forgiving each other if anyone should have a grievance against someone, even as the Lord forgave you, thus also you [others]." Now the punch of Paul's admonition hits you: bearing with one another and forgiving one another go together. The text notes the impossibility of "getting along" with others without the presence of genuine forgiveness.

Throughout my 28–plus years as a minister, more people in and outside the church have asked me questions about forgiveness than any other subject. It seems that forgiveness is always the needed "thing" in our lives. If the truth were known, we all want others to extend forgiveness to us to a greater degree than we are prepared to give forgiveness to others. Who has not thought or said any or all of the following sentences: "I cannot forgive him." "If you knew what she had done, you wouldn't forgive her either." "It is easy for *you* to talk about forgiveness. What do you know of *my* situation?" The questions multiply and the pain compounds and relationships are left broken, wounded, and seemingly beyond repair.

Perhaps we need to hear again Paul's words: "forgive each other." The Greek word translated "forgive" is the verb *charidzomai*. The root of the word — *charis* — is, as a noun, the word "grace." Let's read it that way: "Grace each other." To forgive, it seems to me, is the giving and receiving of grace. And what is grace? Grace is unmerited favor. Simply put, the wrongs we have done to others and those wrongs inflicted upon us are often deeply painful and always leave emotional scar tissue. We can choose to nurse our wounds, replay the tapes of wrongs done against us and revisit the hurt again and again, but healing only comes when grace does its healing work.

Why am I asked about forgiveness so often? Because forgiveness is always the needed thing in our lives. We need to receive it and yes, we need to give it. When Diana, the Princess of Wales, tragically lost her life in an automobile accident, we witnessed the outpouring of grief and love from the British people and much of the world on a scale that defies measurement. Of the many memories we all have of Diana — some deeply spiritual, others revealingly carnal — one keeps coming back in my mind as a parable of our human condition in need of God. You will remember that during the days following her death, the media kept replaying video clips of those moments when Diana touched common people — some who were dying, others in abject poverty and destitution. Such tenderness and compassion from royalty was unlike anything we had witnessed in recent history. Why did we warm to Diana, even though multiplied millions of human beings never met her, touched her, much less experienced her presence physically?

My answer to that question is that all of us — commoners that we are — long to have someone who is "royal" relate to us on the basis of our common humanity. We warm to one in whose life we perceive greatness who would stop, take the time, and touch us with even the most fleeting of handshakes or touches. For all of us who long for such a touch, I have good news. As members of God's new community in Christ, we have become members of the King's family; royal blood has made us one with the eternal sovereign Lord of all creation. This sovereign King, whom we have met in Jesus Christ, calls us to "grace each other" by giving and receiving the one gift that can set free the wounded heart and the bruised relationship, the royal gift of forgiveness. To "bear with" others is to practice the reality of grace in its most radical form: the giving and receiving of forgiveness.

The compassionate new community is one in which we "bear with" each other, "forgive" each other, and yes, find ourselves clothed "with love." In fact, Paul says "above all" — meaning, "this is the most important thing!" — "clothe yourselves in love." Love is the "insider" virtue we learned in the last chapter that bubbles up again here. The new community which learns to get along with each other and which practices the giving and receiving of forgiveness, will experience the clothing, "binding together" power of *agape* love. Unlike shallow water feelings, *agape* does not come and go depending upon the situation, circumstances, or personalities within the community. *Agape* is not a feeling to be savored, but a fact in which we have found and continue to find life. John gave us love's best definition when he wrote: "For God so loved the world, God gave his one and only Son" (John 3:16).

The contemporary Church — Protestant, Catholic, and free church Evangelical — is drowning in the shallow waters of this age for many reasons. Perhaps at or near the top of the list is the fact we talk, teach, and preach about love far more than we practice it, even among ourselves. According to every poll on record in recent years, American adults overwhelmingly agree with the statement "I believe in God." What church and synagogue numbers are telling us is, American adults don't have the same belief in the multiplied thousands of institutional expressions to belief in God — churches, synagogues, mosques, and so forth.

What gives?

Many have laid the "blame" — a word I do not like — at the feet of the media and that faceless, formless, hard-to-define foe we call "Hollywood." Others blame the Supreme Court's decision to ban government sponsored prayer in public schools. Still others mete out righteous rhetoric on "liberal" theologians, universities, seminaries, and other easy targets in firing range. Now, the culprit of choice is postmodernism or post-Christendom or some other word with "post" in front of it.

Being a member of the Baby Boomer generation, I refuse to do what my natural, boomer instincts cry out that I do: Lay the blame with others. No, I must accept my portion of the blame as must every person who claims membership in the new community of the Church. Our society is disintegrating before our very eyes for reasons, some listed below, which all impact each other.

(1) *We have refused to be "salt and light" in a world of tasteless, ever darkening humanity.* The very word "secular" carries with it the hard-to-die myth that at one time, society was "sacred" or at least gave polite and even deferential acceptance to things godly. Such thinking is jaundiced at best and outright blind at worst. There has never been a time when God's new community values have been held sacred by any majority sampling of humankind. Jesus calls us to be "salt and light" in the world because he knew "the world" would always be moving toward putrefaction and darkness. Enshrining Jesus' virtues in law or believing such virtues can be

required of the human family has the effect of lulling us into a corporate complacency best illustrated by the 1500 years of "Christendom" only now coming to an end.

(2) *We have refused to model love within the new community of faith under the lordship of Christ.* We have talked of love, written of love, sung of love, even dramatized loved in countless pageants, plays, and worship services. What we have failed to do is live out love in our relationships with persons of differing race, culture, sexual orientation, and political ideology. Love, as we have defined it, is getting along with people who look like us, talk like us, believe like us, work like us, worship like us, sing like us, and generally keep Jesus at a safe and manageable distance like us. The more risky sides of love — racial reconciliation, seeking economic and political justice for the oppressed, gender equality, radical forgiveness for wrongs — have been neatly avoided or labeled as "liberal."

(3) *We have refused to speak out the love of God in personal evangelism and mission.* The legacy of the now dying age of Christendom is the separation of life into manageable "sacred" and "secular" realms. In doing so, we consigned sacred work mostly to holy men and women. Evangelism and mission, so we reasoned, was the work of the paid clergy, missionaries, and others who would do such work for modest wages, while the rest of humanity worked hard and paid for the sacred work deemed important. What happened to love? It got misplaced in the division of labor.

Paul's summons to the Colossian Christians is a "ding-ding-ding" bell saying "*Helloooooo!*" to contemporary believers. Practicing the corporate virtues of forbearance, forgiveness, and love is not optional in the new community in Christ. They are required and cannot be silenced by referendum. The gift God gives us for practicing these virtues is, of course, the abiding gift of "peace." Using the Greek imperative, Paul declared that if these three virtues are practiced, then "the peace of Christ" will "rule in your hearts" — notice the plural — "to which indeed you were called in one body" meaning the community of faith, the Church. The "peace of Christ" is nothing less than God's "shalom" — wholeness, integration, togetherness — resident in the corporate life of the community of faith.

The world — society — the human family — use whatever word you like — still longs for God's "peace." In fact, human beings so ache for authentic, accepting community, they will join up with almost any group that promises to be a community where forgiveness is practiced, purpose is clear, and the giving of self to others is modeled.[7] Only "in Christ" does the human family encounter a community where eternal life is discovered as a gift (no legalism), forgiveness is unconditional (call it grace), and compassion is the defining virtue of the group.

## A Worshiping Community

> And be thankful. Let the word of Christ dwell in you richly; teach and admonish one another in all wisdom; and with gratitude in your hearts sing psalms, hymns, and spiritual songs to God. And whatever you do, in word or deed, do everything in the name of the Lord Jesus, giving thanks to God the Father through him. (Col 3:15b-17)

The final defining characteristic of the new community is the reality of corporate worship. Here again, we encounter dangerous shallow waters where more than a few believers are drowning. Even a casual observer of American Christianity today will have to admit that the experience of Christian worship is undergoing a radical "sea change" in terms of style, length, components, and theology.[8] At the risk of greatly oversimplifying a complex reality in the contemporary church, let me describe two views of the current worship landscape. On the one hand, we find what I call "worship as entertainment." This phenomenon knows no stylistic or denominational boundaries. One can encounter this kind of worship in both liturgical and non-liturgical churches. In some churches, the service is so ordered that only the clergy and choir actually say or do anything. Even the singing of hymns is much the work of those in robes, in front of the people. The responsibility of those who attend is simply to "be there" and take in what is sung and said from those leading. One gets the feeling at the conclusion of the service that those who attended leave the service asking themselves the important question, "What did I get out of the service today?"

On the other hand, you meet the "worship as surprise" factor in many churches. In an effort to address the problem of worship as entertainment, this model seeks to make each service unique, different, participatory, and of course relevant. This goal is reached by varying the worship form each week by adding or deleting elements of the service, including or eliminating a sermon, using familiar hymns or short, catchy choruses, and often including drama as a way of communicating Bible stories and truths. The feeling one gets at the conclusion of this kind of service is something akin to asking the question, "What happened?"

To the degree any Christian worship service fits these two descriptions is one degree further from the reality Paul describes in the verses above. The new community is called to be a worshiping community in which God is glorified by humankind and human beings both individually and corporately are addressed by God. Worship is an experience in which our lives are transformed by God's power to live in God's world as God's people. Let's look closely at five components of authentic Christian worship. If you are drowning in shallow water, perhaps you have ignored these deep water realities of the worshiping new community.

(1) *Thankfulness*. The first component is also the last. Notice I began the reading with the last three words of Colossians 3:15, "And be thankful." Many scholars associate this command with the verses preceding our text. I chose to include them here because Paul ends this section of the letter by summoning the Colossians to see the entire experience of worship as "giving thanks to God the Father." From first to last, worship requires gratitude and it's cousin thanksgiving. Gratitude is the attitude of indebtedness; thanksgiving is the expression of that attitude to God. We worship God because we owe God a great debt. God has freed us from sin (Col 2:13), erased our record of wrongs (Col 2:14), raised us to life with Christ (Col 3:1), placed us in a community where compassion, forgiveness and love are practiced (Col 3:12-14), and given us the hope of heaven (Col 1:5). Worship is first of all not an activity built upon our likes, tastes, or traditions. Rather, worship wells up from a grateful heart.

(2) *The Indwelling Word of Christ*. We worship because in the company of God's people we experience what Paul calls the indwelling "word of Christ." Before we define what he meant, remember Colossians was written before there was the collection of books we call "The New Testament." Copies of what we call "The Old Testament" were few. So what did Paul mean? From the brief glimpses we have of worship services and sermons in the New Testament, it seems priority was given to telling

the Jesus' story over and over again. The "word of Christ" was the story of Jesus. In Colossians, we read one such account of Jesus' life in the Colossian hymn (Col 1:15-20). By the time Paul wrote this letter, whole pre-Gospel narratives of Jesus' life were circulating in the Church. The "word of Christ" was the repeated telling of Jesus' life, death, and resurrection. Worship that avoids the shallow waters of rote tradition or ever-changing taste anchors its life in Jesus Christ.

(3) *Teaching and Admonishing.* It seems that mutual learning and drawing strength from each other was the third component of first century worship. To "teach and admonish one another in all wisdom" was to remind the Colossians that they had a stake in the experience of worship. Rather than being a "take away" or "What did *I* get out of the service today?" experience, worship rightfully asks, "Did I participate by giving to and receiving from others?" What of "me" was in the experience of worship? Where did others point me to Jesus? Did wisdom — which is always God's gift — inform our learning and affirming experiences? These are questions every Christian must ask before, during, and after the new community gathers for worship.

(4) *The Grace of Music.* Music seems to have had a prominent place in the Colossian church. We spent a whole chapter looking at the Colossian hymn to Christ. Here, Paul brings the gift of music into the light of grace. The words "with gratitude in your hearts" can be literally translated from the Greek, "with grace in your hearts." There is the grace word again. Like forgiveness, gracing each other through music is both a giving and receiving phenomenon. How does that work? From where I sit on Sunday morning, I have a panoramic view of the entire congregation. At times, I notice that people who are living with lingering grief or who have heard awful news about their health or the health of a loved one are finding it difficult to sing. Were it a "normal" Sunday, they would be singing the stars down, but this Lord's Day, the music is not there.

Across the church, however, is a person for whom music has been a dissonant companion for months. For one, grief has been an ominous dark cloud over every horizon; for another, the rejection of all that is moral and decent by a rebellious child has taken all the starch out of life.

And yet, these two are singing today like the grateful, expressive persons I know them to be.

What has happened in the lives of these people? In both cases — one now, the other two weeks earlier — others had to sing the songs for them; the music was not there. So it is when we are able to sing. Music is God's grace-gift to us, enabling the human voice to express glory, awe, praise, love, and commitment to God. Most of the time, we sing; music gives us the vehicle to loose in song the instrument of our voice. Some times, however, we need others to "grace" us with music, all the while believing the song will one day return. Then, we who were silent can grace others with praise. This is one way music adds depth and devotion to our worship. The new community is a company of singing brothers and sisters.

(5) *"In Jesus' Name."* Finally, all worship is "in the name of the Lord Jesus." We worship because of Jesus' life, Jesus' death, Jesus' resurrection, and Jesus' promise to us. To worship in Jesus' name is to place issues of style, format, tradition, music, liturgy, and purpose under his Lordship. In Jesus' name, we no longer ask "What's in it for me?" Rather we ask, "What of me is in it?" We offer our lives, as Paul admonished the Romans, as "living sacrifices" to God, which is our spiritual worship (Rom 12:1-2).

The new community is nothing less than a community where human beings are being transformed into the likeness of Jesus Christ. We are called to be a community where honesty, acceptance, compassion, and worship define our corporate existence and purpose. Living out our devotion to Christ in the new community moves us from the shallow waters of self-defined experience to the ocean depths of authentic, Christian worship and witness. To that last reality Paul addresses in Colossians we now turn.

# Prayer

So much of our lives, our Father, is lived in community. From the family into which we we were born, to classmates with whom we learned the lessons of childhood, to the church where we both saw and heard the story of Jesus. At every point on our life's compass, we find community.

We are ashamed to admit to you that we thoughtlessly take others for granted. This is no more evident than in the community of faith where we worship and serve. Too often, we want our way in church decisions, we argue for our position when we discuss church issues, we vie for the attention of others, hoping to find ourselves in the center of church life. Forgive us, we pray.

As you called disciples to follow you in community, so call us to the journey of faith where others nourish our lives and in whose presence we discover our true selves. Make the church where we have our membership a community of inclusive and transforming worship. Remind us through the work of your Spirit that you are making us the new community of grace and reconciliation through Jesus Christ our elder brother. Amen.

## Notes

[1] See Frank Stagg, *Polarities of Human Existence in Christian Perspective*, Rev. Ed. (Macon: Smyth & Helwys, 1994).

[2] Kathleen Norris, *The Cloister Walk* (New York: Riverhead Books, 1996), 63.

[3] Peter T. O'Brien, *Colossians, Philemon* (WBC 44; Waco: Word Books, 1982), 181.

[4] See, O'Brien, *Colossians*, 181-184; James D.G. Dunn, *The Epistles to the Colossians and to Philemon* (Grand Rapids: Wm. B. Eerdmans Publishing, 1996), 213-216; and N.T. Wright, *Colossians and Philemon* (TNTC; Grand Rapids: Wm. B. Eerdmans Publishing, 1986), 133-135.

[5] Dunn, *Colossians*, 223.

[6] C.F.D. Moule, *The Epistles to the Colossians and Philemon* (The Cambridge Greek New Testament Commentary; Cambridge: Cambridge University Press, 1957), 122-123. In this section of Moule's commentary, he relates Paul's lengthy discourse regarding Israel in Romans 9-11 with Paul's insistence that the new community of the Church is God's beloved people.

[7] See Francis Fukuyama, *The Great Disruption* (New York: Free Press, 1999), where he discusses the sweeping change in society from individuals identifying with large, institutional groups to smaller, more intimate ones.

[8] The best comprehensive treatment of the many changes taking place in American church worship is by Marva J. Dawn, *Reaching Out Without Dumbing Down* (Wm. B. Eerdmans Publishing Company, 1995).

# Living at the Depths

Paul's Letter to the Colossians calls us to experience Christian faith at the depths rather than succumbing to a shallow water drowning. This is not to say that living the Christian life is for high-minded, intellectually aloof, coldly sophisticated snobs. To the contrary. A person who has taken up the task of following Jesus is anything but an aloof, distant, insensitive prude. Look at Jesus. He lived in such close contact with people, he was considered unclean, irreverent, even dangerous. Jesus had table fellowship with outcasts, conversations with whores, physical contact with contagious lepers. Living at the depths is many things. It is not a lifestyle out of touch with real people who live and die struggling with issues like despair, guilt, failure, and rejection.

Let's say for a moment that we accept Paul's critique of our contemporary situation: worship has become more emotive than transformative, prayer is little more than pious pep talks with God, family is on the brink of near extinction, and so forth. Now what? How can thoughtful believers embrace an authentic counter-cultural lifestyle? What are some handles we can use to speak and act, worship and serve, think and reflect from Jesus' perspective, seeing our world through Jesus' eyes, living as givers of grace as Jesus lived? Possible answers to our questions are many. I propose five simple steps you can take right now, today and in the days to come, to begin the journey toward depth living. You may have already taken some of these steps. For my part, I must deliberately engage these five realities daily if I am to keep myself from drowning in shallow water.

## Discipline

The first reality into which we must live to escape the shallow waters of our time is *discipline*. At age six, my parents placed me in the presence of a wonderful woman who became my piano teacher. Polly Mote is a beautiful person in whose life God has placed many precious gifts. At the time — 1959 — she was the organist at our Church. I remember my first piano lesson as if it were yesterday. As I sat at the piano, center of the keyboard, short legs swinging under the bench, Mrs. Mote placed my hands on the keyboard and said the following: "Tim, as you begin to learn how to play the piano, imagine that the tips of your fingers have tiny brains in them, telling your fingers what to play." Tiny brains? For a six-year-old, that was intriguing. From that day forward, so far as I was concerned, and for the next few years, my real brain was only the director telling my "finger brains" what to do.

The weeks stretched into months and the months into years. Today, I still play the piano and enjoy the music and the experience more with each passing year. Often, when I play for a church gathering or a some other function, people ask me how I do it. How does a person play the piano? I'm sure an anatomy professor would give you one answer, a piano teacher another, a poet a third. My answer is simple: discipline. I have long forgotten the hours upon hours I spent glued to the piano bench playing scales, arpeggios, chords, phrases, etudes, preludes, hymns, and any number of other forms of piano music.

I learned at an early age that worthwhile outcomes in life require discipline. Whether it's mastering a new job skill, building a healthy marriage, rearing children to be good students and polite members of society. You name it — nothing of value comes without discipline.

And yet, in the realm of the spirit, so many today act as if spiritual discipline is something to be avoided or worse, unnecessary. A disciplined Christian life is not one that has listened to every tape of every sermon preached by a popular television pastor. Rather, a disciplined life opens the Bible and thoughtfully reads texts daily listening for the voice of God above the noise of contemporary life. Do not get me wrong, I have a tape player and yes I enjoy hearing thoughtful preaching. All the tapes in the world, however, cannot substitute for one's personal reading of the Bible by which one hears the still, small voice of God.

A disciplined life is one that listens for and speaks back to God the heart's thoughts in prayer. Prayer is not so much an activity we "do" as it is a reality in which we live. I find it helpful to read the Scriptures and pray them back to God. Monastic communities through the centuries to this very day pray through the Psalms every 30 days. The 150 psalms of the Bible are spoken out in the community's worship as an experience of prayer.

A disciplined life says "No" to some of the junk food served up by our society and "Yes" to more nourishing food. Such spiritual food as sacred music, the poetry of Donne, Wordsworth, Eliot, Yeats, Dickinson, and others nourish the soul. The writing of George Herbert, Frederick Buechner, Dorothy Sayers, Teresa of Calcutta, Julian of Norwich, Teresa of Avila, Brother Lawrence, Thomas Merton, Max Lucado, Herbert O'Driscoll, and so many others are God's gifts across time and space to feed the hungry heart. A disciplined life is a reading, listening, thoughtful life. Sad indeed is the believer whose only spiritual nourishment comes once a week from a faithful pastor or Sunday School teacher. These dedicated servants are offering excellent fare, but who can survive on one meal a week! The disciplined life summons the courage to turn off the television, put down the tabloid gossip rag, and read the witnesses through whom God has blessed God's people across the years. A pastor–mentor gave me sage wisdom years ago: When you are through reading, you are through.

Music is another gift from God a disciplined person accepts. So much of contemporary Christian music is only the loud blaring of worn out clichés, blasting across thumping drums and loud guitars from voices whose diction makes it impossible to hear the shallow words wrapped inside boring tunes. Yes, there are thoughtful Christian composers and artists today, but they are few. The discipline of nourishing your soul may require you to listen to music that has endured the test of time, rather than tunes that must navigate the test of ratings. Long after the current "hot" contemporary Christian artist is forgotten, Bach's "B Minor Mass" or Mozart's "Requiem" will still be nourishing the human soul. You say, "I can't handle long hair music." Okay. I'm not saying you must. I am suggesting that many drown in the shallow waters of insipid music that is more noise than nourishment. Music can deepen the spiritual life and fill the caverns of the soul with glory. Whether or not we allow God that opportunity often rests in the CDs we buy, the radio stations to which we tune, and the hymns, choruses, and songs we learn.

Disciplined worship — both private and public — is required of all who long to live at the depths. Colossians reminds us that worship includes others. The community of faith is a worshiping, God-glorifying reality. Refuse to become a slave to the "whatever comes along" mentality. For your sake and the sake of your family, make weekly, corporate worship with other believers as normal in your life as breathing. Find time each day for private, quiet worship with God. Five minutes alone with God daily is better than 20 minutes alone with God weekly. The discipline of daily worship deepens your understanding of God's presence and invites you to live aware of God's grace throughout the day.

There is a final discipline often ignored among contemporary Christians. I speak of the discipline of sacrificial service. In our feel good, me first society, few in the Christian family are living out their Christian faith in the context of sacrificial service to others. We are strong on coming to Church, being "fed" by the preacher and "blessed" by the music, finding faithful friends among the family of God. We glory in Christian "fellowship" where we hear no cursing, see no obscenity, and feel no discomfort.

Where we are woefully short today, dangerously playing in the shallow waters of emotional, feel-good Christianity, is in fulfilling Jesus' command to feed the hungry, clothe the naked, visit prisoners, attend to the sick, touch the lepers. In real terms, this means being Christ's presence at a homeless shelter, praying with and holding the hand of a homosexual dying of AIDS, being a surrogate dad to a boy or girl whose father has abandoned them, living with less, giving more, that others may simply live. The discipline of service is absent from most Christian lives. If our nation is to hear the Gospel, if Jesus' life and love are to break through barriers in our society, discipline will have to mark out the living of our lives in the new century in visible, tangible, life-changing ways.

This was at the heart of Paul's message to the Colossian believers. Smitten by the glitter and intoxicating sensuality of Roman culture, they had unconsciously been seduced by a diluted version of the Christian faith that majored on feelings, was fascinated by the mysterious, and defined "real Christianity" by what one did not do — "do not taste, do not touch, do not handle" — rather than building relationships with non-Christian members of society to introduce them to Christ. For the Colossians, discipline was one of the absent realities in their church.

Discipline does not happen without the will. No one but you will hold you accountable for being a disciplined person. The first reality calling us to live at the depths is discipline. Be a disciplined person and watch how God enlarges the interior spaces of your life and multiplies your life in service to others.

## Trust

We are not a very trusting society. Witness the rise of gated communities, the installation of ever smarter security systems, the fear in most parents' lives who must leave their children at a daycare facility day after day. Trust is in short supply in 21$^{st}$ century America.

And yet if we are to live at the depths, we must live in relationship with others in ways that build, nourish, and strengthen trust between men and women, young and old, liberal and conservative, black and white, poor and affluent, pious and profane. But how? How can we live into the reality of trust when we have so much fear, so few trusting relationships, so limited time?

The Colossians struggled with trust in much the same way we do. The Colossian struggle with labeling people, in an attempt to control and coerce uniformity, gives abundant illustration to the low level of trust in that church. We fare no better today. Persons with differing interpretations of what we believe to be significant biblical texts are labeled as either fundamentalist or liberal. We position people theologically or politically in an effort to manage the relationship. Sad to say, too many of our churches are places where the trust level is so low, most people simply keep their mouths shut, attend the services, and hope they will be left alone.

I have seen this so often in the churches I have served and between Christian brothers and sisters in other churches. Gone are the days when we trusted each other so much we could "speak the truth in love" without fear of being rejected or worse, ostracized. As pastor, I know the pain of rejection experienced when church members are so passionate about their theology, their positions, their rights, their whatever, they almost avoid any contact with me or other members of the church who may see a situation from a differing perspective.

Of this I am certain: there can be no Christian maturity without authentic, risky, honest, sacrificial trust given and received between fellow believers. You can mask trust with phony smiles and even firm handshakes, but you cannot manufacture trust with the raw material of superficiality, disdain, arrogance, cynicism, and fear.

So what do we do? In a word, we dare to swim in the direction of the deep water. It's risky and fraught with the possibility of failure, but Christian maturity requires trust to be shared between believers. Here's a suggestion. If you are having a disagreement — maybe even an unspoken disagreement between yourself and your minister, a fellow church member, a Christian friend in another church, or even you spouse or child — start by including your struggle in your conversations with God. The hymn is right: "Have we trials and temptations? Is there trouble anywhere? We should never be discouraged. Take it to the Lord in prayer." Begin your journey toward trust on your knees.

Second, find a person you trust and who trusts you and ask them to pray for you, even with you, about your struggle with trust. For many people, the problem is not some hostility with a church member or disagreement with a minister, but rather a gnawing uneasiness expressing honestly one's understanding or interpretation of any number of issues. For example, I have known Christian brothers and sisters who were the closest of friends who could not discuss certain subjects. Politics, abortion, music, heaven, hell, homosexuality, racial equality, taxes, denominational issues are but a few of the many pressure points in relationships. Confide in a trusted friend and ask that person to pray with you about your need to be more trusting.

Third, put your prayers to work. Find time to be with a friend with whom you disagree on a certain issue. Begin the conversation by asking him or her to pray with you and then say, in your own words, "I've need to talk with you about _____ for a long time, but have not trusted our relationship enough to do so. I've been praying about this and only ask that you listen to me, allowing me to share my feelings. I'm not asking you to agree with me. Agreement is not the goal of this conversation. Rather, I need to convey where I stand on this issue, believing our relationship has more trust in it than I have realized."

I cannot guarantee success, but in my experience, such a conversation has always been far more redemptive, healing, and healthy than I imagined. Friendships deepen, our faith is strengthened, the future is more open and promising when we build trust. You may discover that your friend really needs to share something with you that has been a burden for years. Your ability to take the first step may very well be God's gift to move your relationship to new depths of meaning and joy.

In conclusion, trust is a word whose reality flourishes when more trust is exchanged. When you bear your soul to another person, your trust must be met by that person's commitment to guard your feelings carefully. What hurts and destroys trust more than anything I know is when a person's sacred struggles are taken from a private meeting and reported to others. Often, such reporting is not done to honor the person, but rather to cast doubt upon the person's faith, integrity, or character. Christian maturity demands trust. To live at the depths is to respect other's sacred struggles as you expect them to respect yours. Such is the gift and power of trust to deepen the Christian life.

## Grace

The logical next reality as we live at the depths is grace. In my experience, the needed thing in most of our lives is more grace. Guilt, failure, sin, disappointment, hurt, grief, loneliness are but a few of the human conditions that cry out for grace. And what is grace? Simply put, grace is God's "Yes" to the human soul. Grace is God's affirmation of who we are, regardless of what we have done. More times than not, we do not need someone to tell us we messed up. We know it, God knows it, others know it. Grace is always the needed thing.

Through the years God has given me to engage in pastoral ministry, I can tell you the many times I have failed God, others, the church, and myself. No pastor walks on water; we all have feet of clay. There have been times when I have disappointed people who placed their trust in me. I have said the wrong thing at the wrong time, or the right thing at the wrong time, or the wrong thing at the right time and my words have been more pain, more hurt, more sorrow than hope, joy, or love.

And yes, I know how church members can disappoint and wound a minister. I have experienced this pain from time to time and borne it with fellow clergy across the years. Times are when, unknowingly, a minister fails to be his or her best self. There is no excuse for insensitivity, rudeness, or stubbornness. And yet, if a minister serves a church long enough, he will deliver on all of the above and more. Ministers have bad days, experience depression, know loneliness, find themselves inadequate to meet the demands of the job. Even the ablest of ministers breaks down, expresses some insensitivity, says the hurtful thing from time to time.

But when that happens, church members have the opportunity to extend grace to the minister even as they at times need grace from the minister. I have experienced such grace from church members and know in the depths of my soul what a gift it is to be redeemed, forgiven, accepted, graced. Unfortunately, like all ministers, I have known the pain of not receiving grace when I needed it most. The social slights, the non-invitations to be in a pastoral role for weddings, funerals, or calls in times of illness all give witness to the inability — perhaps only in that moment — to give grace to the one person in the church who may need that grace the most — the minister.

Grace has no exclusive ownership, however, with church members and ministers. Perhaps the place where grace is needed most today is in our homes. Husbands and wives, parents and children, have need of far more grace than we can imagine. Any couple, living faithfully with each other across a span of years, knows the hurt that comes when a husband speaks when he should listen or a wife takes over a situation when she should do nothing. Children are in need of grace and often. Being our young, they will disappoint, fail, sin, fall flat on their faces, give up. We who are their seniors would be wise to give grace first and criticism last; to offer a second or third or fifteenth chance long before we issue ultimatums; to say "well done" even if it wasn't done the way we would have done it.

All who live in family take note. Grace is God's "Yes" to the human soul. God needs our voices and our gestures to speak God's "Yes" to the people we love the most. A mark of living at life's depths is the ability to give grace even when we don't feel like it. To go ahead and say "I forgive you. It is not that big of a deal anyway" long before we ever find a glimmer of sympathy or understanding to really believe it.

It is profoundly simple: grace acts first in love and does the thinking thing much later. Imagine what would happen in our families if we would flee the shallow waters of scorekeeping, holding grudges, figuring out how to get even, and simply move toward the deeper waters of grace? Families might be saved, churches might find new life, ministers might really do their best work ever, church members might finally accept the fact their ministers are human and need companions far more than critics.

Grace is always the needed thing in any relationship. Givers of grace are believers living at the depths.

# Renewal

The need for personal, spiritual, and physical renewal is greater today than ever before. We live at gigahertz speed with ever dwindling resources. Still tied to a 24 hour day, we rear our children from one sign-up to another (soccer, piano lessons, swimming, church choirs, karate — have I named your whole list yet?). Personally, we long for time to play 18 holes of golf, but know we really need to get the yard work done, the garage cleaned, the car tuned, the book read, the report finished, the meal cooked, the video returned, the phone messages answered, the dog groomed, the spouse dated, and the parent visited. Time is not on our side. But of course, neither are we.

We live and move and act and work and play as if we are our own worse enemies. And often we are. There are two wonderful words — five letters between them — we all need to learn to say more often. The first is "Yes," the second is "No." We first need to say "Yes" to God and ourselves. To live at the depths requires that life experience regular, disciplined, healthy renewal. That demands a resounding, hearty "Yes" spoken from the depths of our souls to the hard gray matter of our heads. Renewal is not necessarily a three-day weekend attending a church retreat. It may be that, but I suspect for most of us, that is not what we need.

Renewal is often finding small snippets of time in the midst of a busy day to say "Yes" to ourselves. To close the door to our office, turn the lights off, and be quiet for 10 minutes — to pray, to listen, to be — may be God's perfect gift. Times are when we need an evening alone with our spouse or an afternoon alone with our son or daughter. I know Christian men and women who find great renewal in running, swimming, walking, canoeing, sailing, reading, and painting. Renewal gives us the spiritual energy to live in this busy world from the depths of a replenished soul.

We also must find the courage to say "No." The healthiest word some people could utter in their lives is this two-letter denial. To say "No" to another committee job gives you the opportunity to say "Yes" to your husband or your wife. Saying "No" to a promotion may give you the ability to say "Yes" to your health, knowing the promotion would bring with it more stress, more anxiety, more money you may spend on prescription medicine and therapists than time spent with your family. "No" is a good word. Maturing Christians learn to say it without feeling guilty.

Living at the depths in touch with the reality of renewal enables us to live from the depths with spiritual vitality. Are you tired of church? Weary of worship? Worn out from church jobs that take more from you than you have to give? Are friendships more draining than renewing? If the answer to any or all of these questions is "Yes," you may need to get in touch with the experience of regular renewal. Burned out lay people and ministers are ineffective participants in the community of faith. Exhaustion breeds anger and anger destroys relationships and destroyed relationships "crummy-fy" the joy of being a Christian in community with others.

Looking back on Paul's Letter to the Colossians, I imagine this church had lost the ability to find personal and corporate renewal. Paul admonished them to be persons whose lives were punctuated with prayer: "Devote yourselves to prayer, keeping alert in it with thanksgiving" (Col 4:2). Prayer bonded to gratitude is God's prescription for a life longing for spiritual energy. So take time to say "Yes" to God and yourself by saying "No" to other things — maybe even good things — and discover a depth to the Christian experience that will bless your life and the lives of others. Renewal empowers a life to be at its best for God.

# Celebration

The fifth reality into which God calls us to live deeply is celebration. Too many Christians associate celebration with loose living, drunkenness, or immaturity. Why, Christianity is serious business, isn't it? Well yes, if you mean serious in terms of important, meaningful, life-changing. But no, if you believe the Christian life is devoid of joy, exhilaration, praise, happiness, fulfillment, ecstasy. Living from the depths requires healthy, regular celebration. When you think about it, the entire foundation of the Christian life is built upon the fact that God has begun an eternal celebration by raising Jesus from death and giving to him the title "Lord." The resurrection of Jesus is God's affirmation of life over death, hope over despair, victory over defeat.

Paul reminded the Colossians of this in Colossians 3:1-4. In those four verses, Paul punctuates his writing with significant celebratory words. Christians have been "raised with Christ" and as such, Paul commanded, "set your minds on things that are above." Why? Because "you have died and your life is hidden with Christ in God." The end of all this is that we who believe "will be revealed with [Christ] in glory." Let the celebration begin! Christian believers have much to celebrate. Death is defeated. Christ is alive. There is a greater reality called eternal life awaiting all who are in Christ.

Here is a great truth undiscovered or ignored by many Christian believers. Living from the depths is not energized by heavy thinking, serious Bible study, ponderous prayer, wrestling with the deep things of the faith. Not at all! Rather, living from the depths erupts from a life made new and being made new by the risen life of our Lord Jesus Christ.

Too many believers today are drowning in shallow water. Left to ourselves, life will grind us down one dripping problem at a time. Unchecked and out of touch, we will settle for simple, shallow, ineffective, even destructive solutions to life's struggles. God's gift to believers is the opportunity to live authentically counter-cultural. Many within and without the Church today are drowning in the shallow waters of the 21$^{st}$ century. More seem content to "get by" rather than daring to "go on" into deep, daring, thoughtful living from the depths.

Choose another way. Choose to live the Christian life following Jesus as Lord. Dare to ask the hard questions and live in community with others who will ask them with you. Refuse the easy answers that satisfy the emotions but leave the mind bankrupt and the heart empty. Be a Jesus person who lives so joyously, so purposefully, so deeply, that others will share with you the community of faith where amazing grace is experienced and genuine newness of life in Christ is given and received. Flee the shallow water of this age and live at the depths.

# Prayer

Loving God, giver of every good and perfect gift, author of life, Father of our Lord Jesus Christ, summon us by your Spirit to live fully in the depths of your love. The shallow water of our time has left us gasping for breath. We are depleted by our work, exhausted by recreation, bored by entertainment, frustrated with faith, lonely in relationships. Ours is a cry for help.

Come within and around our lives this day with winsome grace. Call us to move into the deeper waters of nourishing spiritual discipline and renewal. Grant us the courage to flee the tepid, dangerous, shallow water of cheap living where we have kept others, even those closest to us, even you, at a destructively safe distance. Give us ears to hear your invitation to grow into the full person you long to make us by your power.

God of unending patience, bring us to a fuller maturity which alone can bring us to a fuller humanity. Make of us and with us the new community that practices risky love and daring forgiveness through Jesus Christ our Lord. Amen.

# A Short Reading List

Augustine, *City of God.*

_____. *Confessions.*

Brother Lawrence. *The Practice of the Presence of God.*

Bunyan, John. *Pilgrims Progress.*

Calvin, John. *The Institutes of the Christian Religion.* 2 Volumes

Foster, Richard. *The Celebration of Discipline.*

Kelsey, Morton. *Reaching.*

Mother Teresa. *The Simple Path.*

Niehbur, Richard. *Leaves From the Notebook of a Tamed Cynic.*

_____. *Christ and Culture.*

Norris, Kathleen. *Amazing Grace.*

Stagg, Frank. *Polarities of Christian Experience in Biblical Perspective.*

Teresa of Avila. *The Interior Castle.*

Tillich, Paul. *The Shaking of the Foundations.*

_____. *Systematic Theology.*

Wesley, John. *Journal.*

Willard, Dallas. *The Divine Conspiracy.*